DANCE RESEARCH

The Journal of the Society for Dance Research

Volume XXV Number 2 Winter 2007

Editor: Richard Ralph

Published by Edinburgh University Press

The Art that all Arts do Approve:
Manifestations of the Dance Impulse in High Renaissance Culture.
Studies in Honour of Margaret M. McGowan

Contents

Cover: A posture at the barriers from Pistofilo (1627).

T0371007

Subscription rates for 2008

Two issues per year, published in summer and winter

		UK	Rest of World	N. America
Institutions	Print or online	£90.00	£100.00	$200.00
	Print and online	£112.00	£125.00	$250.00
Individuals	Print or online	£45.00	£50.00	$100.00
	Print and online	£56.00	£62.00	$124.00
Back issues/ single copies		£30.00	£33.00	$66.00

Ordering information

Requests for sample copies, subscription enquiries and changes of address should be sent to Journals Department, Edinburgh University Press, 22 George Square, Edinburgh EH8 9LF;
email: journals@eup.ed.ac.uk

All issues prior to 1990 are available from the National Resource Centre for Dance, University of Surrey, Guildford, Surrey GU2 5XH.
Tel: 01 483 259316

Editorial Introduction. Margaret M. McGowan: Pioneer of Academic Dance Research

Margaret McGowan has been closely associated with all editorial aspects of the scholarly journal *Dance Research* almost since its first issue in 1982. For most of the life of the journal she has served as Assistant Editor, involved in the development of its editorial policies, the establishing of its reputation for high standards, and its gradual encompassing of the full range of dance research activity. The years of the journal have been years of considerable expansion within dance studies and research, throughout which Margaret has remained a highly respected and stable point of reference to scholars from widely differing backgrounds.

In recognition of her contribution to the journal in its twenty-fifth year and her contribution to dance research more generally, this special issue has been planned to reflect the range and quality of her work, and that of others working in the early modern period – both dance scholars and specialists in cognate disciplines. The principal focus for the issue is the period with which Margaret has been professionally concerned, French culture in the sixteenth and seventeenth centuries. It is ironic that this work – with all that Margaret and her professional career has stood for – has done so much to support the development of dance studies in Britain: a development that has not been found in France itself.

This is not to say that the quality of her research has failed to attract the admiration of French scholars – or their formative support. André Chastel (a Professor at the Sorbonne), in introducing the 'companion study' to Margaret's first book, Marie-Françoise Christout's *Le Ballet de cour de Louis XIV* (published in 1967), showed a very keen appreciation of the respective and very different strengths of these two works. For in her work, published three years earlier, Margaret had evinced an interest in the political context of dance, in seeing ballet as the product of a culture, an interdisciplinary form that resonated with the political aspirations of the time; she was less interested in dance as spectacular entertainment, and the production side of ballet.

The roots of this precociously modern emphasis in her work are, doubtless, partly innate and partly the result of early influences upon her. The young Miss McGowan was an undergraduate at the University of Reading, which, at that time was distinguished by the presence of such important scholars as Frank Kermode, J. B. Trapp, and Donald Gordon, at an early stage of their academic careers; there, she developed an interest in interdisciplinary approaches, and in looking at the connections between painting, music, theatre, dance and décor. These interests were encouraged further by her experiences at the University of Strasbourg, where she spent a year of her university course and took a French degree. She found this vibrant and forward-looking border city, imbued with both French and German culture, a place of stimulation and varied artistic and intellectual activity. The lively atmosphere of Strasbourg assisted her in widening her sympathies and seeing connections between the visual and performing arts and between them and the culture from which they arose.

She thought carefully before deciding where to apply her scholarly attention, identifying two periods that lent themselves to her interdisciplinary and politico-cultural approach: the transitional period at the end of the sixteenth century and the beginning of the seventeenth century, and the *fin-de-siècle* period at the end of the nineteenth century. She chose the earlier option: in this period, French literature had absorbed the classical heritage 'but was not sure where it was going' – it was a 'melting pot' – the arts were in transition before they found their 'pure' form.

Margaret McGowan embarked upon her doctoral research under the supervision of Frances Yates, the formidably learned *grande dame* of the Warburg Institute (University of London). Frances Yates initially proved to be a rather idiosyncratic supervisor. Given her scholarly predilections, Miss Yates would always be seeking to find cabbalistic mysteries – 'unseen meanings' – concealed in the material being investigated by her student, who would have to insist, repeatedly, that there was 'nothing there'. But once Miss McGowan started to produce written drafts, Frances Yates showed herself to be an acute and constructive reader of the work, and she made an important contribution to it from that point.

Margaret has retained close links with the Warburg Institute throughout her career and has identified D. P. Walker as another major influence upon her from an early stage. As her career developed she was to acknowledge major debts to three other great collections, the Bibliothèque Nationale; the Louvre (where Rosaline Bacou in the Department of Prints and Drawings, and Sylvie Béguin in the Department of Paintings have been especially valued colleagues); and the National Museum in Stockholm, where she has had much support from Per Bjurström.

When she started her work there was nobody else undertaking scholarly research primarily focused on dance in the early modern period – and precious few, if any, in other periods: and in this respect alone Margaret has been a very significant pioneer. There was some help from musicologists, who were interested in music in the service of ballet. Historians also took her work seriously, and it was Jean Jacquot, of the CNRS (le Centre National de la Recherche Scientifique), 'the grand old Renaissance specialist' as Margaret calls him, who was the first to patronise her work and to usher her into the wider world of scholarship. He invited her to contribute at his conferences in Paris, and there she met people who took her – and her work – seriously, showing an interest in what she was doing.

By the time I met her, in 1974, Margaret McGowan's academic career had already taken her to the Universities of Strasbourg and Glasgow where she held lectureships in French from 1955–1964, before moving to Sussex. Her doctoral thesis had been published some ten years earlier, in 1963, as *L'art du Ballet de Cour en France, 1581–1643*.

First impressions are usually not deceptive: and when I paid her a visit in search of help in orientating myself in my own doctoral studies, what I noted at the time has remained an accurate picture of the Margaret whom I have known fairly consistently in the decades since then. Few words are wasted, and the advice is given freely, firmly and with a pinpoint sense of focus. Because of the quality of what is being offered, it is evident that selection is being made from a very copious store of information, and that a ruthless economy (and self-discipline) is employed in both expressing and illustrating what is being offered. It is a habit of mind that accords well with the requirements of senior academic administration – and Professor McGowan has served successfully as Deputy Vice-Chancellor at the University of Sussex and as Vice-President of the British Academy, and led many academic reviews of major departments and institutions over the years.

The bibliography published at the end of this issue, indicates that Margaret's years of higher administration and academic leadership have been combined with the production of a constant stream of academic publications, books as well as articles, which bear witness to remarkable skills of time management and organisation. Her London flat, located close to the British Library, has been a place of constant weekend resort for both Margaret and her husband, Sydney Anglo, himself a distinguished Renaissance historian. Margaret's contribution to the development of the dance research culture in Britain, continental Europe and beyond, has been of great significance, and her own writing therefore represents an important contribution to dance history.

Many of the most prominent dance scholars of the younger generation in Britain and the United States have a strongly theory-based approach to their work – in many cases drawing upon the theoretical structures, vocabularies and debates of French theorists. Needless to say, Professor McGowan is fully conversant with these approaches but has chosen not to employ them extensively in her own work. She feels that theory is less appropriate to the early modern period than it is to dance studies within the twentieth-century. The attempt to relate modern critical theory to early dance gives a wrong impression of the status of dance in its period. In sixteenth- and seventeenth-century dance the focus is upon the individual performance within the group. The art historian Sarah R. Cohen has it right, in Margaret's view. She finds Professor Cohen's discussion of dance in a slightly later period, in her book *Art, Dance and the Body in French Culture of the Ancien Régime* (CUP, 2000) more interesting, addressing, as it does, how the body displays itself in a political framework. Theory of the type represented by Foucault and his peers is more enlightening in the later modern period, Margaret feels. Of course, she is aware that her view is not universally accepted – and she enjoys discussions around these differing opinions and finds interest and stimulation in the work of those, like Mark Franko, who advance them.

When this *Festschrift* was in preparation, Margaret originally submitted a version of her bibliography limited to her work within a specifically dance context. The fuller bibliography, which is attached, exemplifies the breadth of her interests, including, as it does, works on Montaigne, Ronsard, La Fontaine, Racine, Corneille, Molière, John Donne, drama, poetry, opera, aesthetics, music, numismatics, historiography, and the survival of the classical tradition. This generosity of reach is significant, not only as reflecting Margaret's understanding of dance as integral to a widely experienced cultural and intellectual milieu; but also as facilitating an approach to dance itself and a representation of it in scholarship, that is 'fully human' – an activity with physical, aesthetic, spiritual and intellectual components, undertaken by complex individuals and societies, with many resulting dimensions, be they political, personal or cultural.

This breadth in Margaret's focus also demonstrates her equilibrium as a person and as a scholar: she is able to take account of and to weigh the respective significance of varied facets bearing upon the phenomenon of dance. She lacks therefore the distorting and narrowed gaze that can afflict dance purists when they remove the activity from its context and dwell exclusively, disturbingly, and somewhat unhealthily upon it as something isolated from its setting. Margaret's approach is one we would do well to mark carefully as dance becomes a study very much in its own right.

In a more personal sense it is interesting to speculate on the extent to which Margaret's scholarly approach is embedded in the high Renaissance period in which her scholarly life has been immersed, with its emphasis upon wide learning and accomplishment effortlessly displayed in a courteous way within a civilised social environment. Certainly, it would be hard to think of anyone involved in dance who has a higher sense of vocation to the selfless service of those who have followed her. This issue represents token repayment for all she has contributed to dance as a scholar, teacher, supervisor, examiner, administrator and editor, and a measure of the respect and affection in which she is held by her colleagues.

The Barriers: From Combat to Dance (Almost)

SYDNEY ANGLO

The relationships between Renaissance courtly dancing, the art of fencing, and military drill, have recently been much commented upon. This paper explores one particular type of mock combat – the Barriers – where the spectacle moved increasingly close to choreography, but without ever quite becoming a dance itself. After a brief outline of the evolution of the Barriers, the paper concentrates on a number of late sixteenth and early seventeenth century treatises which – rather than the actual combat – all stressed the importance of the passeggio *and* riverenza, *that is the balletic aspects of the spectacle; and placed great emphasis on grace, deportment, foot placement, and on the need to keep exactly to the tempo set by accompanying music.*

An aspect of Renaissance courtly dancing which has recently attracted scholarly attention is its kinship to various martial activities.[1] Fencing and the evolutions of soldiers on the march, in the drill-yard, and even on the field of battle, are now sometimes regarded as having significant affinities to dancing. Agility, grace, speed of movement, and rapid reflexes, are required of fencer and dancer alike; while the discipline of accomplishing complex group movements with speed and precision seems common both to well-drilled troops and to participants in a *ballet de cour*. Moreover, the popularity of mock sieges in court festivals, together with sword dances such as the *pyrrhic, buffens, morescha, mattachins,* and *barriera* (which, despite its name, had nothing to do with the subject of this study), reinforces the feeling that choreography and combat were interrelated. It has even been maintained that many dancing masters taught fencing and that fencing masters often taught dancing. Unfortunately, the connection between martial and dancing skills is less straightforward. Fencing masters and dancing masters were sometimes, but only rarely, identical;[2] and the history of the various arts – in ballroom, school of arms, parade ground, and battlefield – may best be charac-terised as a series of uneven developments proceeding in similar directions, but generally along parallel rather than convergent lines.

For example, throughout the Renaissance and beyond, masters of arms and teachers of dancing were experimenting with movement notation: but even as late as Caroso and Negri, representations of dancers' postures remained wooden and uninformative as compared with the lively, highly-differentiated illustrations of many Italian and German works on personal combat from the late thirteenth century onwards. Moreover, the earliest attempt in print to record fencing movements diagrammatically antedates the exposition of the *buffens* in Arbeau's *Orchésographie* by fifteen years, and may even have been its source.[3] And there is nothing in Renaissance dance treatises which even approaches the complexity and sophistication of Thibault's analysis of movement in his *Académie de l'espée* (1630).[4] Similarly, Renaissance military theorists were developing the diagrammatic representations of drill, bequeathed to them by Aelian and other ancient authors, into an increasingly complex notational system for drilling large numbers of troops, both infantry and cavalry, enabling them to move in unison and to take up different (sometimes wildly eccentric) formations, like a vast armed and armoured troupe of ballet dancers.[5] Here again soldiers anticipated dancers; and it is also likely that the diagrammatic choreographies for horse ballets, which similarly predated such systems for the *ballet de cour*, derived directly from these military notations.

The characteristic of combat which has, perhaps, most suggested a relationship to the dance is the way in which the violence of early tournaments evolved into various forms of mock encounter suitable for court festivals, not only in the lists but also in the banquetting hall or theatre – in entertainments such as disguisings, masques, ballets, *mummerei*, and *intermezzi* – where a battle might resolve some allegorical debate, and where dancing was invariably an essential component at some stage of the proceedings. From at least the thirteenth century, the tournament had been developing into a spectator sport and, gradually, the haphazard mêlée between large groups of mounted warriors gave way to a formal sequence of various types of combat in which danger was mitigated by the use of heavier armour, lighter weapons, rebated lances, and blunted swords; and by the introduction of the tilt which separated the combatants thus preventing collision and increasing the likelihood that lances would snap rather than penetrate. Valour was tempered with discretion: contests were regularised; rules were imposed; and ritualistic and spectacular elements were stressed.

THE BARRIERS: FROM VIOLENCE TO COURTESY

Chivalric combat at the *barriers* merits study because, within the space of little more than a century, it epitomised the evolution of all those activities generally subsumed under the generic title 'Tournament'. At one end of the story knights engaged in mock combats scarcely distinguishable from real battles; at the other, gentlemen leaped about, tapping each other with flimsy laths. And just as the introduction of the tilt and counterlists had effectively reduced the perils of jousting, so, towards the end of the fifteenth century, foot combats were similarly restricted by a wooden bar or gate, over which knights fought with staff weapons or swords. The obstacle prevented bodily contact, diminished the area to be defended, and reduced the variety and strength of the blows.

The *Barriers* was notionally related to attacking or defending fortified places and it may even have retained some military significance in the seventeenth century, as can be seen in a treatise by Flaminio della Croce (1617), where the

Fig. 1. Mobile barrier from Flaminio dell Croce, *Theatro militare* (1617).

barrier is a heavy but portable spiked wooden obstacle and is recommended as cheap, easy to make, and very effective in defending narrow passes or gateways (see Figure 1).[6] The genesis of the sport is sometimes said to be a subterranean combat fought over a fence when English and French soldiers met in the mines at the siege of Melun in 1420.[7] But it is impossible to link this isolated episode to the first tournament (thus far identified) where there is evidence for such a contest – *la barrière perilleuse* at Sandricourt in 1493.[8] The knights were all

Fig. 2. Barriers at Sandricourt (1493).

fully armed but could only thrust at each other over the height of the bar which separated them (see Figure 2). It is unlikely that there were no earlier experiments: but we know nothing of them.

Initially, before rules were clearly drawn, nasty things could happen. Just a year after Sandricourt, in a tournament at Aire, the barrier itself was barely waist high and, during the axe combat, Bayard smashed his opponent's ear. Then, when the victim fell to his knees, the 'good Chevalier' rushed around the barrier and forced the dazed knight to kiss the earth 'whether he would or no' – conduct which would later have been regarded as a flagrant breach of etiquette.[9] This was not an isolated incident, and ways were sought to mitigate the risks.[10] Precautions multiplied. Articles of combat sometimes forbade the use of two hands on the sword, and contestants were forbidden to touch the bar, thrust with their swords, or seize an opponent's person or weapon. The note of caution was especially evident at the diplomatically sensitive Field of Cloth of Gold in 1520, when it was not desirable that injury should befall either French or English knights supposedly enjoying each others' company.

Instead of a hard-fought chivalric contest, the *barriers* was developing into an exercise or social game. As early as 1538, at one convivial occasion at Brussels, it was said that 'some took more hurt with the cups than at the barriers with cutting of the sword';[11] and by the beginning of the seventeenth century, the *barriers* even appeared among the sports promoted at the new University of

Fig. 3. Barriers at the University of Tübingen (1600).

Tübingen as part of the education of young gentlemen (see Figure 3).[12] More significantly, it quickly became popular as a spectacle within a spectacle – that is as part of some semi-dramatic entertainment – as, for example, in the debate between Love and Riches at Greenwich in 1527, or between Wild Men and Amazons in Munich in 1565.[13] Men who were serious about their fighting were displeased. Brantôme, that lover of violence and gossip, jeered at the ineffectual barrier fighting of 'our knights of the Court'; and, by 1642, the Spanish fencing master Narvaez felt that even women and children could play the game. A master of arms must needs be astonished, he sneered, at the weakness of the lances used in this exercise and disgusted at the posturing of frightened combatants who kept close to the barrier for protection and even colluded one with another: saying quietly that 'there must be some give and take'.[14]

THEORISTS

Because movement and weapon-handling were so circumscribed at the *barriers*, few masters of arms bothered with it. However, from the closing decades of the sixteenth century, a few writers did comment on the subject, and their views are revealing. The earliest was, perhaps, Alessandro Rossetti (1571) whose paradoxical coupling of show and the avoiding of affectation was typical of what was to follow in treatment of the *barriers*.[15] Federico Ghisliero (1587), for example – despite his assertion that chivalric exercises must imitate 'the truth' of battle – was similarly concerned more with appearances than with fighting. Knights must never go to extremes: their movements should be natural, 'as much with all

Fig. 4. Foot combat postures from Ghisliero (1587).

the body as with the parts thereof, and always without any affectation'; and, when entering the lists, their deportment must be graceful yet lively, so that they do not look like statues. In his emphasis on artificial Aristotelian categorisations, insistence that truth lies in the middle way, and abhorrence of affectation, Ghisliero followed Castiglione; and, although the greater part of his book offers an original and business-like treatment of fencing, the section dealing with the *barriers* conveys a sense not of knightly endeavour but rather of the elegance which characterised masques and *ballet de cour* (see Figure 4).[16] And this emphasis becomes even more marked in the work of seventeenth-century theorists.

Bartolomeo Sereno (1610) asserts that no knight should appear in the lists without some ingenious *impresa*, and that special attention should be paid to the decoration of armour and clothing.[17] He makes little attempt to analyse combat; and, with regard to sword fighting, his main concern is that knights with strong arms should not use weapons too heavy for feebler opponents to cope with, and that the blows of an adversary should be treated with a show of contempt. Sereno does not like strokes aimed downwards because they might hit the barrier itself, which is, he says, 'an ugly defect' (pp. 141–2). And, most perplexing for the knight, there is the problem of what to do if he drops his sword. Owing to the closed visor, it is impossible to see the weapon on the ground and, if the knight starts to grope about for it, 'as it were in the dark', he will simply make everybody laugh. The best thing, therefore, is to feel for it with the feet and then pick it up, so 'losing only a small space of time' (pp. 149–50). Loss of sword is clearly not as important as loss of face.

Weapon skills interest Sereno less than ensuring that courtiers have appropriate devices and mottoes, suitable assistants, and a fine appearance; that they will observe the correct etiquette for every stage of the spectacle; shun affectation; and enter the lists with gravity and in strict tempo (p. 128). Especially important is the *riverenza* to the ladies present. Knights must not, as when dancing, lead with the left foot and incline towards the ladies' left which is the 'abode of the heart'; but must lead with the right foot, bowing towards the right, whereby (since that side represents strength) the knight shows his humility (pp. 132–3). Sereno has much advice for a knight entering the lists and marching to the barriers. On no account is he to show affectation because the ugliness of that vice is sufficient to diminish the praise which his valour might otherwise merit. He must avoid unseemly movements such as unnecessary stretching or bending. He must not walk stiffly as though he cannot bend his legs; nor cower, bound or leap; nor keep twisting his head around; nor stick his chest out as though he wishes to fight with his paunch. He must move his legs 'with just measure'; bending the knees as appropriate; placing his feet 'with lightness'; and always face his adversary (pp. 134–5).

Sereno notes that, since, in combat at the *barriers*, knights can only be attacked above the waist, any armour worn below that height is superfluous and hinders the agility which is the principal desideratum. This had, in fact, long been the general rule, and illustrations of *barriers* from the mid-sixteenth century usually show knights protected from the waist up but, from there on down, clad only in hose or breeches (see Figures 5 and 6). This, for Sereno, is crucial. In recent years, he complains, the introduction of great breeches [*calzone*] has quite driven out the use of hose [*calza*]. And he exhorts the knight to eschew this new-fangled fashion: 'because the proportion and the strength of the leg is very much better seen with hose than with great breeches which completely cover the firmest part, that is the thigh, and when worn with armour make an ugly sight (p. 121).

Nine years after Sereno's agitatation about thighs, Giovan' Battista Gaiani published a treatise devoted entirely to the *barriers*.[18] He has, he tells us, performed and taught to the applause of great princes, knights of quality, and spectators throughout Italy and, in his view, foot combat – the 'exquisite summit of art' – has reached a perfection far beyond anything known earlier. Its purpose is to display elegance; to provide knightly recreation; to give relish to the prince; and, most of all, to serve the ladies. Its actions should, therefore, 'never pose a danger to life'. On the other hand it does bring practical advantages in warfare by making the knight's body nimble and accustomed to wearing armour which, says Gaiani, can be so oppressive that 'more have been conquered or killed in war by their own arms than by the weapons of the enemy'.

He has a little to say about handling pike and sword: but recommends that the staff should be gripped near the *calcio* (or heel) almost at the terminating spike and held close to the middle of the chest in order not to lose 'too much of the length of the pike, which brings disadvantage in striking' (p. 23).[19] This grip reveals the kind of staff Gaiani has in mind – a feeble little wand whose weight

Fig. 5. Barriers at Vienna 1560, by Hans Lautensack.

(even when held at its extremity) would not impose any strain upon the delicate knight. Indeed, if the staves were prepared according to Gaiani's instructions, they would have been especially brittle for he advises that they should first be bound together at the top, bottom, and middle (so that they cannot warp), and then dried in an oven. This ensured that they are easy to break whereas, were the wood left green, the staves would bend rather than snap – an ugly and damnable effect (Gaiani, p. 59). Gaiani also advises against holding the staff too tightly lest the point tremble: which is the reason why some knights thrust badly and fail to break their pike.

He has little confidence in the skill of his courtiers, and suggests that they should aim their blows at the opponent's left pauldron or gorget: 'because it is very difficult to hit the head, and when you do it is more by luck than by

Fig. 6. Barriers from the Valois Tapestries.

judgement' (pp. 23–4). Yet he still ponders the relative merits of a heavy or light *celata* (close helmet) before reaching an Aristotelian decision that it should be on the heavy side of middling because it has to resist so many blows! He is anxious, too, about the fastenings of the visor, recommending that 'the rivets and locking screws' should be of 'double strength and well tempered'; and he stipulates that the helmet should be lined with wax rather than sponge to prevent any 'hollow re-echoing [*ribombo*] in the brain'.[20] And even then one cannot be too careful. The armourer, with all his tools and spare parts, must be on hand throughout the combat (and especially at the conclusion when the helmets are being removed),

Fig. 7. Pike virtuosity from Antonio Vezzani (1688).

because some knights have almost died when the screws of their helmets have been so smashed that it has been impossible to open the visors because the armourer had already gone off home.

Gaiani's main concern, though, is with deportment: especially when entering the lists. Arm gestures must be accompanied by appropriate foot movements, often with the right foot in the air, and synchronised to 'fill the eye wonderfully' – an anticipation of the pike virtuosity later elaborated by Vezzani (1688) (see Figure 7).[21] According to Gaiani, the whole *giustezza del corpo* and understanding of *tempo* resides in these movements (p. 4). And he is precise as to the placing of the feet, likening the correct method to the 'manner of the crane': placing one foot on the ground while simultaneously raising the other; and, at every pace, pausing a little. This makes an 'effect of wonderful bravura', especially when a man is in armour (p. 6). There must be no disorder, no unseemly movement of body, head or limbs, and no 'shaking or other balletic actions' [*tremoli ò altri atti ballareschi*] – a hostile comment on the dance at odds with the general tenor of the treatise in which there is a great deal about foot placement, and even advice that the shoes for foot combat should be soled with the leather reversed (that is with the pile outside) in order that they might grip better. Gaiani reprimands those who raise their feet too high and thus show the soles of their shoes, or who wave their bodies about, 'which is a great affectation'; and, unlike Sereno, he thinks that knights should *not* bend their knees but should proceed 'as elephants do, carrying the legs and thighs completely unbent, which shows bravura and intrepidity'; presumably a sort of goose-step (p. 19). On the other hand, when taking one's place at the barrier, it is a good idea to flex the knees a little as if to test the firmness of the ground: 'which confers marvellous grace and shows a mighty disposition' (p. 32).

The *passeggio* into the lists is the heart of Gaiani's treatise, for this is when the knight is most exposed and must, therefore, make his mark. His steps must be 'slow, grave, and executed with art and gallantness'; and his gestures must demonstrate 'grace, lightness, nimbleness and mastery both of himself and of the pike'. In short, his entry must 'fill the eyes of the bystanders' because, while there are many who cannot appreciate the technicalities of combat, everybody understands and admires a knight's deportment.

When several knights make their entry together, they must keep to the beat of the drum, and Gaiani provides an example of five bars of music with crosses to indicate the steps which begin on the second beat to ensure that everybody starts simultaneously (pp. 44–8). This is no simple matter for, in all the principal cities, Gaiani has seen knights make a mess of things by running ahead of the correct tempo with hasty steps. Moreover, although all was properly done at the marriage of the Duke of Savoy's daughters (presumably the festivals of 1608) and at the court of the Duke of Mantua, not all drummers do their job correctly.[22] Knights must keep in time, turning their heads *secondo il concerto*, yet in such a way as to appear 'heedless' of the sound – a reminder of Castiglione's studied nonchalance – and must hold their bodies straight. This creates an effect of *intrepidezza e di bravura* but is not, apparently, anything to do with serious fighting.

Nor, curiously, is the last and most elaborate work devoted to the *barriers*. At nearly 600 pages of text, Bonaventura Pistofilo's *Il Torneo* is a prime example of muscle-bound pedantry.[23] The author, who is fond of Greek and Latin etymologies, likes to define even the simplest of terms (taking eight pages merely to explain what combat at the *barriers* might be); and he relentlessly subdivides every part of his subject. There are, for instance, eight chapters on the judges; five on cartels; eight on the *padrini*; five on the *Maestro di Campo*; five on the use of the drum for which Pistofilo provides four pages of printed music illustrating how knights are to march in step (pp. 118–19, 121–2); and eight on the *Passeggio* into the lists, which is an action of 'greater consequence than almost all the other acts put together' (p. 156). Certainly, it seems more important than the long discussion of the *Combattimento*, which is largely concerned with the knight's gestures, and which makes clear that the weapons used are fake and merely for show.[24]

One of Pistofilo's observations concerning the drum is that its beats must be clear and intelligible and that the knight must adjust each pace and each movement of his weapon in time with those beats, and 'according to the same rule that is observed in dancing the galliard' (p. 115). Certainly, as he later makes clear, the knight must not lift the points of his feet, like those who cut capers when dancing , and must especially avoid dragging and shuffling the feet as when dancing *il cannario* ('strisciando e stropicciando, come si balla il cannario'). On the contrary, the feet should be raised cleanly, as is fitting for the gravity of a knight (pp. 161–2).[25]

The most revealing part of Pistofilo's treatise is his Third Book which consists of 117 full-page copperplates, intended primarily to elucidate the chapters devoted to combat. Each plate depicts a single knight adopting some pose, and each is described in a facing page of text. These engravings, executed by Giovanni Battista Coriolano, are attractive enough: but few suggest serious combat. They are generally rather effete; and, in the only illustration showing a staff being broken, it looks as though it has been prepared, as Gaiani had recommended, in an oven. The knight himself seems somewhat at a loss (see Figures 8 and 9).

CODA

In 1629 Antonino Ansalone published a general treatise on knighthood, *Il Cavaliere*, which encapsulates the entire process of the mutation of the knight from warrior to courtier and, thereby, provides a context within which one may see how far the *barriers* had moved away from combat and towards the dance.[26] Ansalone's knight, like Castiglione's courtier before him, has to be good at everything. He must be a skilled horseman, fencer, swimmer, and hunter; he must know how to handle firearms; he must be knowledgeable about mathematics, letters, poetry, theatre, music, and history; he must know how to tilt, fight in the open field, run at the ring and quintain, perform in carousels and the cane game; and know about bull-fighting and horse ballet. He must also take part in the *Torneo a piedi* which, significantly, is nothing more than a gentle combat at the *barriers*; and he must be seen as an active participant in *spettacoli e nelle mascherate*.

Ansalone has a lofty view of the *barriers*, because its performance depends entirely upon a knight's own *virtù* and valour rather than that of his horse (p. 125). However, it soon becomes clear that little valour is involved when Ansalone discusses the use of the pike which, like Gaiani's oven-dried weapons, is merely a flimsy lath designed to snap. Similarly, the sword for combat at the barriers must be light, and the object is to strike the crest of the opponent's helm, not the opponent himself. Only horizontal blows are permitted, either forehand or backhand; and even here there are those who 'through weakness of arm, not being able to hold the weight of the sword easily in the hand, are obliged to deliver short blows' (p. 130).

Like his predecessors, Ansalone's principal concern is with the entry into the lists. The knights proceed 'to the sound of drums and other instruments', and display fantastical devices to show that, beneath their physical appearance, there resides a 'most beautiful and gentle spirit'. Posture and the manner of the *riverenze* must be carefully regulated. Affectation is the great enemy. So, too, are ugly movements 'which are noisome and displeasing'; and, in order not to fall into such abominable defects, knights are enjoined to recall what was written on this matter by Alessandro Rossetti who had stressed the importance of moving body, arms and legs, *al naturale e con vivacità* (p. 127).[27] Ansalone also notes that it is of no small profit to the knight to know how to dance because, 'as said the Count Baldassare Castiglione, one must observe a certain majesty tempered with graciousness [*leggiadria*], and an airy sweetness of movement, with time and measure'. The knight is enjoined to avoid excessive speed and complicated steps which go beyond decorum; and Ansalone is at pains to define *la leggiadria*. This quality is, he says, a certain observation of natural law governing both the whole

T E R Z O.   385

Figura XXXII.

Fig. 8. A posture at the barriers from Pistofilo (1627).

T E R Z O.

Figura LXXVII.

475

Fig. 9. A surprise! A staff broken from Pistofilo.

body and the individual limbs, so that no movement or action is performed without rule, measure, or design.

It is apparent that all those writers concerned with combat at the *barriers* repeat the same basic ideas. They all display an obsession with the *passeggio* and the *riverenza*; with grace, deportment, and foot placement; with laws governing movement; and with the need to maintain a fixed tempo set by accompanying music. They all stress *sprezzatura* and the need to avoid affectation; yet all favour an artificial style of movement. And none goes beyond a cursory glance at fighting techniques. The original martial exercise – when knights, though hampered by a barrier, actually tried to hurt each other – is brushed aside. Bearing in mind that these views mark the work of theoreticians who were writing about combat within the lists as the outcome of a chivalric challenge, then we are, I think, entitled to speculate as to the balletic nature of the *combats à la barrière* in banquetting hall and theatre with which students of *ballet de cour* and court masques are more familiar. The combat never quite became a dance. But it came very close.

NOTES

1. See especially, Kate Van Orden, *Music, Discipline, and Arms in Early Modern France* (Chicago and London, 2005); Barbara Ravelhofer, *The Early Stuart Masque. Dance, Costume, and Music* (Oxford, 2006).
2. For example, of the forty-three dancing masters listed by Cesare Negri, *Le Gratie d'Amore* (Milan, 1602), pp. 2–6, only four are said to have been teachers of fencing. P. Brioist, H. Drevillon, P. Serna, *Croiser le fer* (Mayenne, 2002, p. 140, assert that Arbeau and Saviolo taught both fencing and dancing. But this is unlikely: although John Florio, *Second Frutes* (London, 1591), p. 119, does refer to Saviolo as 'a good dancer'. A striking late example of the combination is the work of Johann Georg Pasch who wrote not only on fencing and wrestling, but also on dancing.
3. Henri de Sainct Didier, *Traicté contenant les secrets du premier livre de l'éspée seule* (Paris, 1573), combines a primitive tracking system with figurative representations; and, as the student Capriol assures his teacher, Arbeau, in the *Orchésographie* (1588), 'fencing has already acquainted me with all these gestures'.
4. On Thibault, see Sydney Anglo, *The Martial Arts of Renaissance Europe* (2000), pp. 73–82 etc.
5. See J. R. Hale, 'A humanistic visual aid. The military diagram in the Renaissance', *Renaissance Studies*, II (1988), pp. 280–98.
6. Flaminio della Croce, *Theatro militare* (second edn: Antwerp, 1617), Figure 5, pp. 147–9.
7. Jean Juvenal ds Ursins, *Histoire de Charles VI, Roy de France*, ed. Michaud and Poujoulat (1836), pp. 559–60.
8. A. Vayssière, *Le Pas des armes de Sandricourt* (Paris, 1874).
9. *History of Bayard*, tr. Loredan Larchey (1883), p. 60.
10. At the *barriers* held in Paris to celebrate the marriage of Louis XII and Henry VIII's sister Mary in 1514, the French, anxious to humiliate their guests, introduced a German giant to beat up the Duke of Suffolk who, however, leaned over the barrier and 'by pure strength tooke hym about the necke, and pomeled so about the hed that the bloud yssued out of his nose', See Edward Halle, *Chronicle*, ed. H. Ellis (1809), pp. 571–2. In 1519, at the *barriers* at Noseroy, knights were still being knocked to the ground by blows with the butt end of the lance, or severely wounded by sword cuts to head and hands. See B. Prost, *Traité du duel judiciare* (Paris, 1872), pp. 244–5, 247–8.
11. *The Lisle Letters*, ed. Muriel St Clare Byrne (Chicago and London, 1981), V, No. 1109a.

12. Johann Christoph Neyffer and Ludwig Ditzinger, *Illustrissimi Wirtemburgici ducalis novi collegis quod Tubingae quam situm quam studia quam exercitia accurata delinateo* (Tübingen?, 1600).

13. See Halle, pp. 722–4; Giuseppe Bertini, *Le nozze di Alessandra Farnese. Faste all corti di Lisbona e Bruxelles* (Milan, 1997), pp. 41, 65.

14. Brantôme, *Oeuvres complètes*, ed. L. Lalanne (Paris, 1873), I, p. 234; Luis Pacheco de Narvaez, *Advertencias* in D. L. Orvenipe, *Armas y desafíos* (Madrid, 1911), pp. 278–81.

15. Alessandro Rossetti, *Operetta del combatter alla barra* (Naples, 1571). I have not been able to consult this work, but its contents are summarised in Carlo Padiglione, *Di Alessandro Rossetti e di un suo libro alla barra* (Naples, 1864).

16. See S. Anglo, 'Sixteenth-century Italian drawings in Federico Ghisliero's *Regole di molti cavagliereschi essercitii*', *Apollo* (November, 1994), pp. 29–36.

17. Bartolomeo Sereno, *Trattati del uso della lancia a cavallo, del combattere a piede, alla sbarra et dell'imprese et inventioni cavalieresche* (Naples, 1610), pp. 119–20.

18. Giovan' Battista Gaiani, *Discorso del tornear a piedi* (Genoa, 1619).

19. For more serious advice, by Giacomo di Grassi, on handling staff weapons, see *Martial Arts of Renaissance Europe*, pp. 161–5.

20. Cf. Pietro Monte, *Exercitiorum atque artis militaris collectanea* (Milan, 1509), Lib. II, Cap. 96, where the knight is advised to stuff wax into the front of his helm to protect the head from the 'noise and clangour' of the blow.

21. Antonio Vezzani, *L'esercizio accademico di picca* (Parma, 1688).

22. *Discours de ce qui s'est passé aux nopces de Infantes de Savoye. Avec les courses et tournois faits à la Barrière, tant à pied qu'à cheval* (Paris, 1608).

23. Bonaventura Pistofilo (Bologna, 1627).

24. The head of the polaxe, for example, is of wood painted to resemble metal and must not be too hard – so that it can be easily broken (pp. 60, 258).

25. Like Sereno, Pistofilo does not like the knight to bend his knees when walking, nor does he approve of sticking out the paunch.

26. Antonino Ansalone, *Il cavaliere descritto in tre libri* (Messina, 1629).

27. See above, n.15.

'Rules for Design': Beauty and Grace in Caroso's Choreographies

JENNIFER NEVILE

This article examines the changes Fabritio Caroso made to his choreographies from his first treatise Il ballarino *(1581) to those from his second,* Nobiltà di dame *(1600), as well as the terms Caroso used to refer to these changes and the significance that these terms had for him. While modern scholars have discussed these changes as evincing an increased interest in symmetry by Caroso, the dance master did not employ this term in his treatises at all. The terms he did use were closer to the earlier concepts of Vitruvius's* symmetria *and of Leon Battista Alberti's* concinnitas. *The analysis of his choreographic changes demonstrate that Caroso was not particularly focused on symmetry in the modern sense, that is, in increasing the number of mirror or rotational symmetrical spatial patterns in his revised choreographies. What we do see in Caroso's revised choreographies is an increased interest in balance and repetition, the arrangement and number of elements, and a concern to provide a theory or rules for designing choreographies that were articulated and written down, and conformed to the prevailing theory of beauty in the other arts, in order that his choreographies would also be judged to be perfect and to epitomise grace and beauty.*

On the title page of his revised dance treatise *Nobiltà di dame*, published in Venice in 1600, Fabritio Caroso speaks of his 'newly corrected' dances that have been improved since their first appearance in *Il ballarino*, 1581 (see Figure 1).[1] Modern dance scholars have discussed Caroso's improvements as evincing a 'belief in symmetry', and as 'an abundant concern for symmetry – equal representation for each foot in the dance movement'.[2] Caroso, however, never used the word 'symmetry' in his treatises. Therefore, in order to fully appreciate the changes he made to his choreographies and the results of those changes, it is necessary to outline exactly what terminology Caroso used in *Nobiltà di dame* and what these terms might have meant for him. As will be demonstrated, the changes introduced by Caroso into *Nobiltà di dame* were closer to earlier concepts found in the writings of Vitruvius and Leon Battista Alberti than to our modern-day concept of 'symmetry' which tends to imply mirror symmetry. From an analysis of the choreographies from the two treatises, we can see that Caroso's corrections primarily involved introducing balance, repetition, and regular shapes, rather than an increase in the number of mirror or rotational symmetrical spatial patterns. Caroso's changes show affinity with the wider sixteenth-century

Fig. 1. Title page of *Nobiltà di dame* (courtesy of the Library of Congress).

intellectual discourse on the arts, as he too was concerned to fashion his choreographic creations so that they conformed to the contemporary ideal of beauty.

VITRUVIUS, ALBERTI, AND CAROSO'S TERMINOLOGY

When Vitruvius used the word *symmetria* in his architectural treatise *De architectura* the term had several meanings, each related but slightly different.[3] For Vitruvius *symmetria* meant either 'rules for design', 'good proportions', 'style' or 'of the same size and shape'.[4] Vitruvius's usage of *symmetria* survived for centuries.[5] In Leon Battista Alberti's treatise on architecture *De re aedificatoria* (1450) Vitruvius's wide-ranging term *symmetria* was replaced by the term *concinnitas*: 'an aptness of the parts within a whole so that nothing can be added or taken away, be decreased or enlarged, or be differently placed.'[6] Alberti's *concinnitas* resembled Vitruvius's *symmetria* in that it was 'the task and aim of *concinnitas* to compose parts that are quite separate from each other by their nature, according to some precise rule, so that they correspond to one another in appearance'.[7] By the end of the sixteenth century in both Italian and French dictionaries the word 'symmetry' (*simmetria/simmetrie*) had narrowed its meaning somewhat from the usage of Vitruvius and Alberti, and meant the 'due proportion of each part to the other in respect of the whole'.[8] Vitruvius's sense of 'good proportion' and 'of the same size and shape' are encompassed by Florio's and Cotgrave's definitions.

As noted earlier, in *Nobiltà di dame* Caroso does not use the Italian term *simmetria* (symmetry) at all. When talking about the dances he has corrected Caroso uses the phrases *vera theorica* (true theory) and *regola terminata*,[9] as well as *belle regole* (beautiful or fine rules), *vera mathematica* (true mathematics) and *perfetta theorica* (perfect theory).[10] The exact meaning of *terminata* is not entirely clear, but is seems to imply that his rules are ones that are limited or bounded or defined by the requirements of his 'true theory'.[11] Thus *regola terminata* could be seen as close to Vitruvius's *symmetria* when he uses this word to mean 'rules for design'. Certainly the whole sense of Caroso's terminology is that he is applying rules determined by a theory of design to his choreographies so that they will be perfect and will be seen to epitomise grace in the eyes of the onlookers (*sarà alli astanti gratiosissima vista*).[12] Thus in Caroso's vocabulary there are resonances not only of Vitruvius's rules for design, but also of Alberti's *concinnitas*, in that it is the arrangement, number and placement of elements, in Caroso's case choreographic elements, that results in true beauty.

CAROSO'S CHOREOGRAPHIC CHANGES

By considering Caroso's comments on the 'badly made' (*mal fatto*) dances from *Il ballarino*, and what he has done to alter these choreographies, it is possible to identify these design rules. Feves has arranged these rules into three groups: the rules of polite society, the rules of art, and the rules of nature.[13] Choreographic changes dictated by the rules of polite society mainly occur at the beginning of the dance. In his earlier treatise sometimes the woman starts the dance on the man's left hand side, rather than on the man's right hand side, the place of honour, whereas in the later treatise the woman always starts on the man's right-hand side. The rules of art as identified by Feves included changes such as the creation of new steps with the names of poetic feet – the *spondeo* and *dattile* steps, for example – or with the names of architectural columns, as is the case for the *corinto* step, or the addition of musical note lengths to the names of the dance steps. For example, in *Il ballarino* the steps, generally speaking, come in two forms, *grave* or *minima*. In *Nobiltà di dame* the steps are called *lunghi*, *breve*, *semibreve*, as well as *minimi* and *semiminimi*.

The rules identified by Feves as the rules of nature, refer to the alternation of the feet.[14] In *Nobiltà di dame* Caroso insists that if one foot is already forward, it cannot be used to start the next forwards movement: it is the foot that is behind that must do this. Thus forwards movements must always begin with the back foot, and movements travelling backwards must begin with the foot in front.[15] Caroso was also concerned to correct choreographic sequences or *passeggi* so that if they first started with one foot when repeated they started with the other foot. In practical terms the changes that Caroso introduced into his later, revised choreographies, particularly those changes that fall into the category of rules of nature, are what dance historians have identified as evidence of Caroso's increased interest in symmetry; that is, symmetry in the modern sense of mirror or reflective symmetry. I will now look in more detail at Caroso's choreographic changes in order to identify the differences in his choreographic style between his 1581 treatise and that of 1600.[16]

Caroso's own statements as to how he has corrected a particular choreography, because it was badly made in the past, give the impression that the dances in *Il ballarino* were a long string of step sequences within which repeated sections were non-existent. This would be far from the case. Some dances are comprehensively rewritten in *Nobiltà di dame*; others are altered only slightly; and the amount of rewriting does not consistently relate to the number of repeated sequences in the earlier version. Certainly the step sequences in the *mutanze* and the *passeggi* in the *Gagliarda di Spagna* and the *Passo e mezzo* are substantially altered from their earlier, idiosyncratic forms, so that in *Nobiltà di dame* they invariably follow a step sequence beginning on one foot with a repetition of the same step sequence beginning on the other foot. Yet in other dances that Caroso corrected in 1600, their earlier 1581 versions contained quite a number of repeated step sequences. Some of these dances from *Il ballarino* are almost totally rewritten for *Nobiltà di dame*,[17] while in others, also with balanced repetitions of step sequences, very few changes are made.[18]

The *Spagnoletta* for two from *Il ballarino* is one of the earlier dances that are constructed around the principle of repetition, first on one foot then on the other. Each of the five *tempi* (or sections) in this dance has an eight-bar step sequence, then a sixteen-bar refrain. The refrain is itself divided into two eight-bar sections, with each eight-bar section constructed of two four-bar sequences, performed starting first on the left foot and then starting on the right foot; that is, the sixteen bars of the refrain is (4 bars × 2) + (4 bars × 2). Furthermore, the eight bars at the start of the third, fourth and fifth *tempi* are also a four-bar repetition, first performed to the left starting on the left foot, and then performed to the right starting on the right foot.

The *balletto Contentezza d'amore* is another dance from *Il ballarino* that is mostly constructed of short, balanced step sequences, repeated first on the left foot then on the right foot. However, when the step sequences are repeated the spatial patterns are not necessarily repeated as well. Sometimes this happens, as in the first *tempo* of *Contentezza d'amore* where the four *riprese* moving to the left are followed by four *riprese* to the right, retracing the same path. In the second and third *tempi*, however, the repetition of the two *puntati gravi*, two *passi* and one *seguito ordinario* is not performed on the same path at all.

So if the dances from *Il ballarino* contain examples of repeated step sequences, the collection also contains dances that were not constructed around the principle of repetition. For example, in *Il conto dell'orco* and *Alta regina* the refrain is not repeated: it is a single step sequence. In *Alta regina*, however, this single step sequence of the refrain is balanced spatially, in that each dancer returns to his or her starting place by the end of the refrain; that is, the refrain does not cause them to change their position on the dance space. When re-writing *Alta regina* Caroso modified this refrain slightly, leaving the two *puntate* steps – one forwards and one back – but he removed the single turn to the left-hand side that ended with a *cadenza*, replacing these steps with a *riverenza*. He also substantially altered the rest of the step sequences, replacing them in the third, fourth, fifth and sixth *tempi* with new sequences repeated first on the left and then on the right. The non-repetitive or unbalanced refrain of *Il conto dell'orco* disappears entirely in the new version from *Nobiltà di dame*. The refrain is replaced in the first two *tempi* with a sequence of four different steps, each one done once to the left and once to the right. The principle of repetition and balance asserts itself in the third and fourth *tempi* with the couple in the third *tempo* taking right hands and moving slightly to the left-hand side while beginning the step sequence on the left foot, while for the fourth *tempo* the couple begin by taking left hands and move to the right-hand side, beginning the same step sequence on the right foot.

From this analysis one can conclude that there are more repeated step sequences in Caroso's later dances, and that these step sequences tend to be longer in *Nobiltà di dame* than in *Il ballarino*. But does this equate to an increased interest in symmetry? The answer to this question depends on one's definition of 'symmetry'. Caroso's interest in symmetry was far closer to Vitruvius's and Alberti's understanding of *symmetria* than to our modern idea of mirror, axial or translational symmetry. Caroso's *symmetria* consisted of his design rules that needed to be followed when composing a choreography, of which two key rules were balance and repetition. Repetition of the step sequences was essential so that step sequences would be 'of the same size and shape'. Choreographic sections or whole *tempi*, step sequences and spatial patterns also had to be balanced, so that there was nothing that 'needed to be added or taken away, or decreased or enlarged', or rearranged. Principles such as variety, for example variation in the opening positions of the dancers, became less of a consideration for Caroso when he redesigned the choreographies for *Nobiltà di dame*.

The changes made by Caroso in *Nobiltà di dame* do not substantially alter the

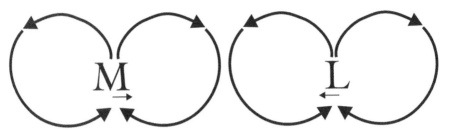

Fig. 2. Symmetrical circling floor pattern in *Contrapasso* from *Il ballarino*.

amount of translational, mirror or rotational symmetries present in the spatial patterns of the choreographies. For example, in the *balletto Contrapasso* from *Il ballarino* a symmetrical circling pattern occurs first to the left-hand side with two *seguiti* left and right, and then to the right-hand side with the same two steps also on the left and the right foot.[19] This pattern is shown in Figure 2.[20] In *Contrapasso in ruota* from *Nobiltà di dame*, however, this passage is said to be 'very false' (*& questo era falsissimo)*,[21] and the steps are altered to two *passi* left and right, one *seguito* left all turning to the left, and two *passi* right and left, one *seguito* right all while turning to the right. Thus when turning to the right-hand side the man and woman now step out on the right foot, rather than on the left foot as previously. The symmetrical spatial pattern, however, has not changed. Each separate floor pattern is still a circle in mirror symmetry.

   In many of the dances from *Il ballarino* the floor path of each dance contains sections of mirror, rotational (or axial), and translational symmetry. A brief analysis of the *balletto Barriera* for two from *Il ballarino* will illustrate the point.[22] In baroque couple dances mirror and rotational symmetry predominate.[23] The symmetry is achieved by the man and the woman moving together at the same time, usually starting on opposite feet. The path of the man is one side of the symmetrical pattern and the woman's path is the other (see Figure 3). In sixteenth-century choreographies the symmetry frequently takes a different form. For example, the couple both start on the same foot, and usually perform the step sequence together. Therefore symmetry is achieved over time when a step sequence is repeated. *Barriera* from *Il ballarino* begins with the man standing at the right-hand side of the woman, not in the customary position to the left of the woman. After a *riverenza* and two *continenze* steps, two *passi seguiti* are performed in order for the couple to changes places. This is shown in Figure 4. These two *seguiti* create a semicircular pattern that is an example of rotational symmetry. The step sequence for the second, third, and fourth *tempi* of *Barriera* are identical, as is the path traversed by the two dancers during these three *tempi* (see Figure 5a), except that the path has moved slightly to the right by the end of each *tempo* by virtue of the two *riprese* to the right, which are not balanced by any step(s) back to the left (see Figure 5b). Thus the symmetry created in the floor plan of the second, third and fourth *tempi* is translational symmetry, both in terms of space – the slight shift to the right – and time.

la Bourée d'Achille.

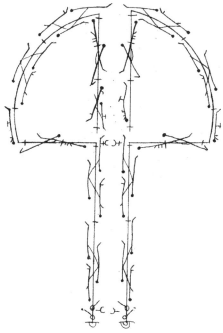

Fig. 3. Example of mirror symmetry in baroque dance. The opening eight bars of Pécour's *la Bourée d'Achille* (courtesy of the Library of Congress).

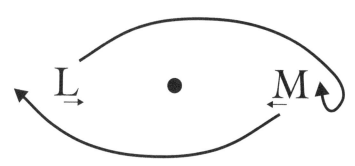

Fig. 4. *Barriera* from *Il ballarino*: Semicircular floor pattern from the 1st *tempo*.

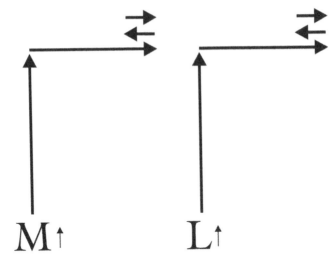

Fig. 5a. *Barriera* from *Il ballarino*: floor pattern of 2nd, 3rd and 4th *tempi*.

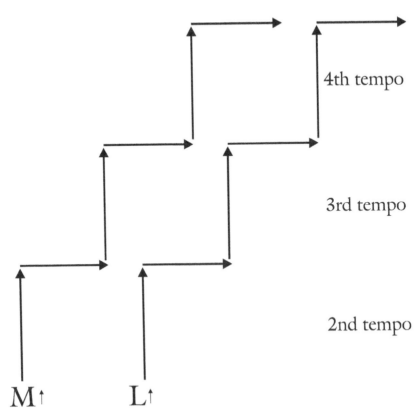

Fig. 5b. *Barriera* from *Il ballarino*: translational symmetry in the 2nd, 3rd and 4th *tempi*.

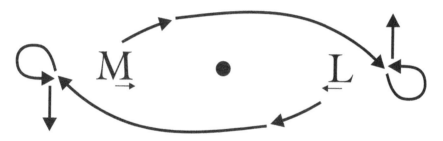

Fig. 6. *Barriera* from *Il ballarino*: floor pattern of 5th *tempo* – rotational symmetry.

Figure 6 shows the complete path of the fifth *tempo*. Each segment of this path is an example of rotational symmetry around a central point. In the last *tempo* of *Barriera*, the seventh, the woman repeats what the man has just performed in the sixth *tempo*. The man's movements towards and away from his partner are repeated by the woman, thereby creating rotational symmetry over time. The floor patterns of *Barriera* are common to many *balletti*, and so are the forms of symmetry that they create. These forms and the frequency of their occurrence do not appear to increase markedly from 1581 to 1600. Even when the step sequences are not repeated, as in the case of the two *seguiti* near the start of *Barriera*, the path created by the two dancers is still symmetrical in one form or another. It is certainly harder to identify symmetrical passages in the sixteenth-century dances than in baroque dances notated in Feuillet notation, since much of the symmetry in the former is created over time: it is sequential rather than occurring concurrently.

CAROSO'S AND SIXTEENTH-CENTURY THEORIES OF BEAUTY

Thus there does not seem to have been such an increase in the creation of mirror and rotational symmetrical spatial patterns in the late sixteenth century. Certainly there was not the overwhelming concern that was present in baroque dances. What was important in the sixteenth-century *balletti* was not symmetry in the modern sense of 'mirror symmetry', but balance and repetition, and the creation of regular geometric shapes. As Alberto Lavezola confirms in his work *Il ballo* from 1575 where he insists on the geometry and the symmetry of the danced figures,[24] symmetrical spatial patterns were important in sixteenth-century *balletti*, as they were in other art forms in the sixteenth century.[25] But this interest continues throughout the period: it does not increase around the end of the century as opposed to the mid 1550s. What did change was an increasing interest in balance and repetition, the arrangement of elements, and an increasing concern to provide a theory or rules for designing choreographies which were articulated, and written down, and conformed to the prevailing theories of beauty in the other arts.

By refashioning his choreographies in *Nobiltà di dame* Caroso was concerned that his artistic creations conform to the contemporary ideal of beauty: an ideal that was achieved by an arrangement of elements in a way that was well-proportioned, with all the parts harmonising with each other. Caroso wished his choreographies to be perfect,[26] thus epitomising grace and beauty. The sixteenth century produced many written descriptions of beauty and perfection, from Vasari's *Lives of the Painters, Sculptors, and Architects*, to Agnolo Firenzuola's *Dialogo delle bellezze delle donne* (1548), where he says 'beauty consists of grace that comes from the harmonising of several parts'.[27] Pierre de Ronsard was another who held to this ideal, as is illustrated by his description of the paintings of Corneille de la Haye.

When, sire, you look at an excellent painting by the Fleming, [Corneille de la Haye] so well proportioned, where the colours are well applied and the lines well drawn, and whose parts harmonize with each other through a beautiful and ingenious symmetry, all in such a telling way that you are immediately obliged to marvel at it ... .[28]

The 'symmetry' that Caroso was concerned to introduce into *Nobiltà di dame* was not our modern idea of mirror symmetry, but rather a concept much closer to Vitruvius's *symmetria* and Alberti's theory of beauty, *concinnitas*. Just as Ronsard saw the beauty of de la Haye's painting residing in the well-proportioned arrangement of the different elements of painting, all of which were in harmony with one another, so too did Caroso desire to establish rules for his choreographic elements which he could then use to arrange these separate elements so that they would 'correspond to one another in appearance.' Caroso's *belle regole* and *perfetta theorica* are his design rules which render his choreographies such fine examples of true beauty that everyone who sees them performed 'are immediately obliged to marvel' at them.

ACKNOWLEDGEMENT

I would like to thank Graham Pont for reading this article and for his perspicacious comments and suggestions.

NOTES

1. Fabritio Caroso, *Nobiltà di dame*, Venice, 1600. Facsimile edn, Bologna: Forni, 1980.
2. Angene Feves, 'Fabritio Caroso and the Changing Shape of the Dance, 1550–1600', *Dance Chronicle*, Vol. 14, nos 2 and 3 (1991): 166. See also Barbara Sparti, 'La 'danza barocca' è soltanto francese?', *Studi musicali*, Vol. 25, nos 1–2 (1996): 290, and David J. Buch, *Dance Music from the Ballets de Cour 1575-1651. Historical commentary, Source Study, and Transcriptions from the Philidor Manuscripts* (Styvesant, NY: Pendragon, 1993), p. xvii. In her introduction to Ercole Santucci's treatise Sparti has commented that Caroso's 'corrections were according to 'true theory', one aspect being an insistence on symmetry' (Barbara Sparti, 'Introduction' to *Mastro da ballo (Dancing Master) 1614*, by Ercole Santucci Perugino [Hildesheim: George Olms, 2004], p. 89 ft.1).
3. See Marcus Vitruvius Pollio, *De architectura libri decem*, Book 1, chapter 2.
4. George L. Hersey, *Architecture and Geometry in the Age of the Baroque* (Chicago: University of Chicago Press, 2000), p. 101.
5. Hersey, *Architecture and Geometry*, p. 101. See ibid., pp. 101–3 for Hersey's explanation of how in the seventeenth century the word's meaning changed to become closer to the modern idea of mirror symmetry.

6. Joan Gadol, *Leon Battista Alberti: Universal Man of the Renaissance* (Chicago: University of Chicago Press, 1969), p. 108.

7. Leon Battista Alberti, *On the Art of Building in Ten Books*, trans. Joseph Rykwert, Neil Leach and Robert Tavernor (Cambridge, Mass.: MIT Press, 1988), p. 302 [9.v].

8. John Florio, *A Worlde of Wordes* (1598; facsimile edn, Hildesheim: George Olms, 1972), p. 372. See also *A Dictionarie of the French and English Tongues*, complied by Randle Cotgrave, (1611; facsimile edn, Hildesheim: George Olms, 1970), for an almost identical definition of *simmetrie*.

9. 'I'hò corretta con Regola terminata, & con vera Theorica' (Caroso, *Nobiltà*, p. 2).

10. Above the diagram of the dance *Il contrapasso nuovo* are the words 'il Contrapasso fatto con vera mathemetica' (Caroso, *Nobiltà*, p. 241), while at the end of the dance Caroso has written 'finiranno questo Ballo fatto con vera Regola, perfetta Theorica, & Mathematica' (they will finish this dance [that is] made with the true rule, perfect theory and mathematics) [Caroso, *Nobiltà*, p. 243]. For an examination of Caroso's *Il contrapasso nuovo* and the diagram attached to this choreography from *Nobiltà di dame*, see Nancy Kane, 'Architecture and Icon in Caroso's *Nobiltà Di Dame*', in *Proceedings of Twenty-Fourth Annual Conference of the Society of Dance History Scholars, 21–24 June 2001*, compiled by Juliette Crone-Willis, SDHS, 2001, pp. 55–9.

11. Julia Sutton translates *terminato* with the word 'symmetrical'. See Fabritio Caroso, *Nobità di dame (1600): A Treatise on Courtly Dance*, trans. and ed. Julia Sutton (Oxford: Oxford University Press, 1986), p. 343 in the Glossary, and pp. 88 and 158. Feves translates *terminato* as 'limit'. See Feves, 'Fabritio Caroso and the Changing Shape of the Dance', p. 160. Markus Lehner concludes that *terminato* 'means that all steps within one stanza are danced equally often with the left and right foot'. (Markus Lehner, 'The *Cascarda*: An Italian Dance Form of the Sixteenth Century', in *Terpsichore 1450–1900: Proceedings of the International Dance Conference, Ghent, April 2000*, ed. Barbara Ravelhofer [Ghent, Institute for Historical Dance Practice, 2000], p. 16.)

12. Caroso, *Nobiltà*, p. 104.

13. Feves, 'Fabritio Caroso and the Changing Shape of the Dance', p. 161.

14. Feves, 'Fabritio Caroso and the Changing Shape of the Dance', p. 162.

15. See, for example, Caroso's explanation of the *spezzato finto* step (Caroso, *Nobiltà*, p. 57), and in his revised choreography for the *balletto Alta Vittoria*, where he warns the reader that the earlier *ballo* was false, and 'contrary to natural motion' (*è contra moto di natura*) and 'contrary to the rule' (*contra la Regola*), because ending the first *riverenza* with the left foot behind means that one cannot do a second *riverenza* with the same foot, a sequence that he had choreographed in the earlier version of the dance (Caroso, *Nobiltà*, p. 297).

16. For a discussion of the ways in which Caroso altered his *cascarde* in *Nobiltà di dame* from their first appearance in 1581, see Lehner, 'The *Cascarda*', pp. 15–18.

17. The *balletto, Amore Costante*, is one dance that fits into this pattern.

18. For example in the dances *Bassa Honorata* and *Le bellezze d'Olimpia*.

19. Fabritio Caroso, *Il ballarino*, Venice, 1581. Facsimile edn, New York, Broude Bros, 1967, pp. 173r–173v, 'voltaranno alla sinistra, con due seguiti ordinarij ... poi voltando alla destra, faranno due altri seguiti ordinarij'.

20. The path of the man and woman separately is a circle in mirror symmetry, while the paths of both the man and the woman together is an example of translational symmetry.

21. Caroso, *Nobiltà*, p. 285.

22. Caroso, *Il ballarino*, pp. 77v–78v.

23. For a discussion on symmetry in baroque dance, see Ken Pierce, 'Choreographic Structure in Baroque Dance', in *Dance, Spectacle, and the Body Politick, 1250–1750*, edited Jennifer Nevile, Indiana University Press, forthcoming 2008.

24. Alessandro Arcangeli, *Davide o Salomè? Il dibattito europeo sulla danza nella prima età moderna* (Rome: Viella, 2000), p. 114.

25. For a discussion of symmetrical patterns in Renaissance gardens and dance see, Jennifer Nevile, 'Dance and the Garden: Moving and Static Choreography in Renaissance Europe', *Renaissance Quarterly*, Vol. 52, no. 3 (1999): 805–36.

26. 'che dove quella era imperfetta, hoggi questa l'hò ridotta à vera perfettione.' Caroso,

Nobiltà, p. 2.

27. The quotation is from Margaret M. McGowan, *Ideal Forms in the Age of Ronsard* (Berkeley: University of California Press, 1985), p. 161. For an extensive discussion on sixteenth-century views of beauty and how these manifested themselves in Ronsard's work, and on French ideals of the beautiful dancing form, see ibid., pp. 160–250.

28. Ibid., p. 160. The translation is McGowan's.

Fragment of the Sovereign as Hermaphrodite: Time, History, and the Exception in *Le Ballet de Madame*[1]

MARK FRANKO

The fragment in Le Ballet de Madame *(1615) is the Androgyne ballet in which a young Louis XIII on the verge of his majority performs the role of a Hermaphrodite. The analysis reveals the complex iconography of this role with respect to the recent erasure of his succession to kingship after the death of Henri IV in 1610. The presence to social memory of the king's un-mourned corpse is relived in the Hermaphrodite figure, which is also a phoenix. But, this is only possible through the sexual imbroglio of the incorporation of the patriarch's body in that of his successor, a veritable figure of melancholy in psychoanalytic terms. Hence, the hermaphrodite fragment proves important to the political imaginary of absolutism in that we can perceive that the body natural of the king is brought to the fore at the expense of the body politic. The analysis is carried forth through the study of a series of contemporary texts devoted to this ballet and the theoretical background provided by twentieth-century interpretations of baroque power: Walter Benjamin, Louis Marin, Ernst Kantorowicz, and Georgio Agamben. The king as Hermaphrodite shows the bare life of sovereignty and the embodiment of the exception, which is Carl Schmidt's answer to Benjamin's notion of allegory. Hence, the essay brings extensive historical research into dialogue with contemporary theory at the level of the analysis of theatricality as a mode of symbolic action.*

'... [A]llegory uncovers nature and history according to the order of time' – Gilles Deleuze

On 19 March 1615, Louis XIII (1601–43), then fourteen years old, danced the role of a Hermaphrodite in *Le Ballet de Madame*.[2] This article contains a close reading of the ballet's textual sources and a historical contextualisation of its circumstances, putting these in relation to twentieth-century theories of power and representation.[3] Walter Benjamin's notion of the fragment as well as of allegory will be important touchstones of my analysis.[4] I interpret the Herma-phrodite role as Benjamin's 'highly significant fragment'.[5] The ballet scene that claims my attention is fragmentary by virtue of its uniqueness in the repertory as well as by its appearance in a non-linear, if still sequential, performance. I shall argue that the Hermaphrodite scene – the 'Ballet des Androgynes' – is a fragment that should claim a central place in the history of absolutism's political imaginary.[6]

THE KING'S TWO BODIES, ALLEGORY, AND BARE LIFE

In his *The Origin of German Tragic Drama* (1928), Benjamin uncovered the 'disastrous' relationship between authoritarian political power and allegory. Through his analysis of the German seventeenth-century 'tragedy of mourning' (*Trauerspiel*) Benjamin undermined the mythic symbolism of kingship by substituting the model of incorporation for that of incarnation. To reduce his argument to its barest essentials: the techniques of allegory are multi-directional and time consuming; ultimately, they imprint their subject matter with the melancholy awareness of corruption and decay. The presence of death in representations of power entails melancholy whose processes are those of incorporation (internalising the dead) rather than incarnation (embodying power as an eternal principle). To say with Benjamin that the sovereign 'represents history' is to say that the sovereign himself is subject *to* history rather than history's Subject.

Approximately thirty years before the English-speaking world discovered Benjamin, Ernst Kantorowicz's *The King's Two Bodies* (1957) established itself as the obligatory text of reference for questions of the ruler's body in relation to absolutist political power.[7] Kantorowicz's operative constructs of *the body politic* and *the body natural* are founded on the distinction between power's undying nature (incarnation) and the living body's mortality (abjection). His acknowledgement of the necessity for a body natural in the scheme of absolutist power is precisely what makes *The King's Two Bodies* relevant to studies of power and performativity. Yet, Kantorowicz's work, albeit the analysis of a legal fiction, affirmed the mythical aspects of monarchical power without accounting for the compromising costs of embodying those myths. The body natural itself became a convenient fiction in that its melancholy was disavowed.

For Kantorowicz, the role of the body natural is at once to insure power's embodiment and to 'stand aside', as it were, whenever this embodiment could be convincingly construed as the incarnation of a transcendent (and inevitable) force. This emphasis on incarnation removes the exercise of autocratic power from the pressure of historical reality. The cachet of the body politic is that it 'lives' in an untouchable symbolic vacuum with the body natural as its invisible prop. Kantorowicz never sets the abjectness of the body natural into relief as a *value* in itself.

The body can be considered abject simply by virtue of being mortal.[8] Ralph Giesey studied the body natural's abject state in connection with royal funeral ceremony.[9] Georgio Agamben looks at abjection as a limit state of life, or what he calls 'bare life'.[10] Agamben takes exception to Kantorowicz's emphasis on the perennial aspect of the king's body politic at the expense of the body natural's mortal and fallible condition, arguing that sovereignty and bare life are actually co-implicated. Law becomes indistinguishable from life in the sovereign decision characterising the state of exception, a twentieth-century variant of absolutism. The state of exception – nothing other than the state of emergency we are familiar with today in western democracies – signals the withdrawal of power from the law, and the absorption of law into life. This transformation of legal power into personal authority brings bare life into focus as the bio-political counterpart to what Carl Schmitt, Benjamin's contemporary, called 'the decision in absolute purity'.[11]

In the case study I present here, the king's body natural is not a convenient fiction, but stands forth instead as the bare life of sovereignty. I ask how bare life becomes incorporated into the sovereign body itself in its most glorious opportunity for self-display – ballet – rather than being correlated with the sovereign power to decide on the fate of another's body. What, in other terms, are the political stakes of the incorporation of the abject into the sovereign body?

Agamben's discussion of sacred life (and the ambiguity of the term sacred) as corollary to the exception is relevant to my case study because of the way it realigns the relationship between body politic and body natural. Agamben analyses the ambiguity in the term sacred. *Sacer* is 'the originary exception in which human life is included in the political order in being exposed to an unconditional capacity to be killed' (85). The condition of bare life is to be subject to 'the decision in absolute purity', which places it beyond both sacrifice and homicide. The relation of the sovereign to bare life is thus 'the originary "political" relation' (85). Two consequences ensue that are of interest to me here. One is the 'structural analogy' between the sovereign and bare life; the other is sovereignty as a state of indistinction between 'violence and law' (35).

The structural analogy presupposes that the sovereign and *homo sacer* are 'two symmetrical figures that have the same structure and are correlative: the sovereign is the one with respect to whom all men are potentially *homines sacri*, and *homo sacer* is the one with respect to whom all men act as sovereigns' (84). They are thus joined in 'the figure of an action' that delimits 'the first properly political sphere of the West' (84). In the case study below it should become clear that the sovereign (understood here not purely as a function but as a functioning being in the theatrical arena) comprises both poles of the figure of this action. This leads us to the second point. Agamben explains the state of exception with reference to the Hobbesian concept of the state of nature. The exception reintroduces the state of nature into the law while itself representing a zone of indistinction between law and nature.

The state of nature and the state of exception are nothing but two sides of a single topological process in which what was presupposed as external (the state of nature) now reappears, as in a Möbius strip or a Leyden Jar, in the inside (as state of exception), and the sovereign power is this very impossibility of distinguishing between outside and inside, nature and exception, *physis* and *nomos*.[12]

This topological figure is none other than the fold, a figure in which inside and outside are rendered permeable but in which interiority and exteriority are preserved as independent topological moments.[13] As we shall see, what constitutes the complexity of this 'topological figure' is saliently located in the context of *theatricality* itself, which throws tropes of embodiment (and hence certain views of performativity) into disarray. Theatricality is not merely an exemplar of indistinction but a *theoretical figure* in its own right, one that encompasses a form of prophetic thinking, and operates diegetically through incorporation.

CASE STUDY

The occasion of *Le Ballet de Madame* was the marriage of Elizabeth, Marie de Medici's thirteen-year-old daughter and the sister of Louis XIII to the ten-year-old Phillip IV of Spain. The brother and sister performed in the ballet, with Elizabeth portraying Minerva. The marriage celebrated between France and Spain was controversial for contravening the will of the late king, Henri IV, who had been assassinated in 1610. Performed shortly after Louis XIII reached majority in the autumn of 1614, *Le Ballet de Madame* may well have resonated with the loss of the father, and particularly with the unprecedented curtailment of the mourning of his death, to which I shall return shortly. It is a ballet of mixed occasions: it celebrates a marriage, commemorates an untimely and catastrophic death, recalls a suppressed mourning and a premature succession, and marks an accession to majority.

Le Ballet de Madame is composed of a plot-less parade of figures that include Night, clouds, Sparks of Fire (*les Ardents*), Sibyls, Androgynes, Shepherds, and Tritons. Margaret McGowan points out that its lack of narrative interest was compensated for by a new emphasis on spectacle.[14] One can also note the extreme political importance of the ballet, signaled by the unusually detailed description of its spectacular elements published in the chronicle *Le Mercure François*.[15] For example, we learn that the performance was illuminated by twelve hundred white candles, danced on Turkish rugs surrounded by paintings, sculpture and tapestries, had nine children as Sparks of Fire running with four candles burning on their head and a torch in hand, and used clouds to accentuate the dramatic appearance and disappearance of characters. Another text published in *Les Oracles François* indicates that *Le Ballet de Madame* was also the object of a certain cultural anxiety.[16] I end this article with a close reading of that text.

McGowan interprets the ballet as the Regent Marie de Medici's attempt to shore up her own rule and that of her son, Louis XIII.[17] This is underlined by the *Mercure François* account, which makes much of Louis XIII's age: '... [C]ar le nom du Roy de Bourbon, qui contient treize lettres; il avoit treize ans lors que le marriage fut resolu, et il est le treizieme Roy de France du nom de Loys.' ['... The name of the Bourbon King contains thirteen letters; he was thirteen when the marriage was concluded, and he is the thirteenth French King with the name Louis'.][18] The political significance of the ballet is connected to the king's reaching majority some months earlier at the age of thirteen.

The Hermaphrodite role is coordinated in this ballet with the phoenix image of the verse, which is part of an iconographic tradition related to royal succession. Moreover, the phoenix, as Kantorowicz notes, was 'a creature having two sexes, or a hermaphrodite'.[19] This is also to gender the king's two bodies where the female sex would correspond to the body natural. Because of the rebirth imagery of the phoenix the weaker sex of the body natural, from which the new body politic springs, is the father's. Nevertheless, the Hermaphrodite is a singular being with two sexes, played by Louis XIII.

Just as such allegorical imagery was being used in ballet to consolidate the claims to power of Louis XIII, the norms of family, state, and sexual identity were also being consolidated. The marital maxim, as explained by Sarah Hanley, tied the king's sexual identity to his symbolic political function: '[The marital maxim] linked family formation and state building by contractually uniting king and kingdom in a political state marriage likened legally to that of husband and wife in a social civil marriage: *the king is the husband and political spouse of the kingdom.*'[20] Changing iconographic norms for the symbolisation of sovereignty suggest that the marital maxim announces the genealogy of the 'closed self' – *homo clausus*, generally understood as a bourgeois concept – based on stable individual identity.[21] As Dorinda Outram shows in *The Body and the French Revolution*, the body of *homo clausus* implies self-possession and self-sovereignty, 'the drawing of lines between the self and others, between 'internal' and 'external' worlds, and between one body and another'.[22] The hermaphroditic body implies just the opposite: an 'open self' whose exceptionality is in no way constricting to personal identity.

Le Ballet de Madame was staged at the intersection of these conflicting iconographic and political norms. As power drew more consistently on images of the patriarchal father and spouse, the hermaphrodite was becoming compromised as a symbol of political stability. The first court case in France brought against a hermaphrodite dates from 1601, the year of Louis XIII's birth.[23] Biological hermaphrodites were becoming associated with sexual ambiguity, and hence with 'sexual metamorphosis, transvestism, and sodomy'.[24] Kathleen Perry Long finds the hermaphrodite role in sixteenth-century French fiction to be 'a direct subversion of society'.[25]

What made the Hermaphrodite role controversial, then, is the fact that the young king himself performed, and thereby ritually asserted, his power against the backdrop of these shifting norms. While a tension between overlapping iconographic systems could be tolerated, the tension could nevertheless not be ignored. His person was to ground family and state through stable gender ascription. The association of the monarch with a feminine principle weakened the relationship of his power to masculine identity, which was as important as noble identity.[26] The theatrical presentation of ambiguity or duality in the monarch's sexual and gendered identity might well compromise the unity and integrity of his power the ballet was ostensibly engineered to project.

Le Ballet de Madame exists at the heart of a contradiction noted by scholars working on early-modern hermaphroditism. The body natural as a theatrical phenomenon invites identification with 'the maternal principle', following Kristeva, or with 'the feminine', following Christine Buci-Glucksmann.[27] My analysis, however, presupposes no essentialist conception of gender. I understand the gendered figuration of absolutism, and its absolutist concept of being (what

Greenberg calls the 'integrity of being') as a phantasm. I do not think gender was an ontological category historically, nor do I think it is one presently.

Much recent work on early-modern hemaphroditism argues that the legal problem of the hermaphrodite is not sexual duality *per se*, but the hermaphroditic subject's choice of sexual identity in everyday life. A biological hermaphrodite could choose to live as either a man or a woman. As long as s/he plays one sexual role consistently, s/he is not called before the law. Thus, the problem of the early-modern hermaphrodite was not one of the essence of gender *per se*, but of its signs. By the same token, the problem of boys playing women in Elizabethan theatre was that of dissolving male identity under the influence of costume. The focus on signs of gender undermines any notion of an essence of gender. 'If gender could not itself be grounded, it was paradoxically itself one of the main grounds for the distribution of political and legal power'.[28]

THE PHANTASM

Louis Marin theorised the relation of phantasm to reason of state: 'The fête, by its *magic* and in that register, represents more clearly than any other domain the phantasms that animate the reason of state in its principle and project.'[29] For Freud the phantasm is unconscious material entailing the subject's active physical participation, a combination of the nocturnal dream and the daydream, latent content and symptom.[30] Michel Foucault underlines the phantasm's performativity: 'Phantasms do not extend organisms into an imaginary domain; they topologise the materiality of the body ... They must be allowed to conduct their dance, to act out their mime, as "extra-beings".'[31] This is an important point in that it stresses the necessary 'there-ness' of the king's body in ballet. To evoke the imaginary is not to displace the *real* of performance.[32] The imaginary and the real converge in the theatrical, which is the mode of the phantasm.

Marin's reference to magic reminds us that Freud characterised the fantasy of incorporating the beloved lost object into oneself as magical, and typical of melancholy. Freud likened melancholy to an internalisation of the deceased, 'an *identification* of the ego' with the lost object.[33] Incorporation or internalisation is a form of identification that bypasses mourning. If mourning is 'work' that leads to the acceptance of death melancholy is a magical operation that retains the departed within us. *Le Ballet de Madame* refers to a recent history in which public mourning might have, but did not, take place. Melancholy plays a role in the ballet as a socially acknowledged, and in some sense publicly shared, consequence of the elimination of the father's funeral ceremony in 1610. Some background is in order.

THE EFFIGY'S DISAPPEARANCE

In French ceremonies of succession a life-like effigy customarily represented the deceased king. The effigy represented the body politic of kingship in a life-scale, fully clothed puppet.[34] It was initially placed on top of the royal coffin containing the un-embalmed remains of the king's body natural. As the effigy acquired a processional life in the ecclesiastical obsequies independent of the un-embalmed corpse, the effigy asserted the Dignity of the crown in a civil and political sense. This homage to the body politic occurred at the expense of two bodies natural: that of the deceased king and that of his heir, who remained in the shadows.[35] The heir's customary absence from the ceremony rendered him virtually invisible until his predecessor's final interment. The substitution of the effigy for the corpse enabled the funeral ceremony to be prolonged, sometimes for weeks, thus effectively extending the period of the successor's obscuration as well. The official act of mourning thus consigned both the dead king's hidden remains (the body natural) and the living body of his un-anointed successor to a sphere of invisibility and abjection. The effigy, according to Ralph Giesey, allowed the 'body politic' to accede to a palpable 'afterlife'. This occurred as 'the effigy evolved from a simple representation of the deceased on top of the coffin into a magical other-than-mortal body, kept separate from the corpse and treated as though still alive'.[36] Giesey calls this state of affairs 'the thaumaturgical denial that the king had really died'.[37]

The effigy was abruptly eliminated in 1610 at Henri IV's funeral. Hours after his father's assassination Louis XIII, then nine years old, was presented in a *lit de justice* (a ceremonial appearance before Parliament).[38] This ceremony amounted to 'the instant succession of a minor king'. The 'interregnal puppet' was nowhere in evidence, nor did it return thirty-three years later when Louis XIII himself expired.[39] 'The funeral ceremony,' writes Giesey, 'which had treated the royal Dignity in more or less abstract terms yielded to a new ritual, centered exclusively on the person of the living king.'[40] The disappearance of the effigy effectively collapsed the difference between the body politic and the body natural of the king, thus signaling the state of exception.[41]

LE BALLET DES ANDROGYNES

The ten androgynes that allegorise the people of France ('la France et son peuple fidele') are called *Machlyennes*, which derives from the Latin *Machlis* or *Achlis*, meaning mad beast, but also designating an androgynous north-African people.[42] The libretto specifies that the *Machlyennes* were a nation living in the swamps of Triton on the Mediterranean coast of Libya where Minerva is said to have first appeared and been raised. Their connection to Louis comes diegetically, then, through the character of Minerva, whom Elizabeth portrays in the ballet. Although the Androgynes serve thus to introduce the character of Minerva, the verse makes reference to succession:

> Puis, comme si un noeud les mariast ensemble,
> A mesme temps ce zele en un corps les assemble
> Pres le Ciel ou souloit luire son beau Soleil.
> La, chacune, à l'envi, promptement se vient rendre,
> Pour garder le phenix qu'avoit produit sa cendre
> En courage a son pere, et en vertus pareil.[43]

[Then, as if wed together in one knot,
In one body does this zeal assemble them
Near the heaven where his Sun was wont to shine.
Each hastened there to see
This phoenix rising from its ashes
Equal in courage and virtue to his father.]

The father and the son are as if wedded as if in one 'knot' (*noeud*). The *Machlyennes* personify the kingdom as a racialised collectivity that witnesses this fiery union, and the emergence of the son from the ashes of the father.[44] The ballet pictures succession as parthenogenesis and emblematises succession through what Kantorowicz calls a 'queer ornithological dualism'.

A medal was struck after the death of Louis the Just, also known as the French Phoenix, in 1643. Its device weds the phoenix with the sun: 'Le Phoenix naist et s'eleve des Cendres de son pere par l'influence qui luy est envoyée du Ciel et du Soleil' ('The Phoenix is born and soars from the ashes of his father by the influence sent to him from heaven and the sun').[45] The descriptive system of the phoenix comprises heat, flame, and conflagration, not the sun's light and radiance. This is perhaps because the sun emblematises an effect on the public, whereas when iconography shades into performance its interpretation becomes more action-oriented. Consider contemporaneous accounts of royal entries that link fireworks with the nation's admiration of, and loyalty to, the crown.

Or comme le feu ne produit pas seulement la lumière, mais qu'il contient et donne de la chaleur, il sembloit seul capable de bien représenter la disposition des âmes et des coeurs de ce peuple à l'arrivée de ses Souverains.[46]

[Since flame not only produces light but also contains and gives warmth, it was well chosen to represent the receptive mood of the hearts and souls of this people to the arrival of their Sovereigns.]

Why are the people androgynous, African, and danced by women? Why is the racial and gendered Other – 'lost to the heart of the nation', as Anne Anlin Cheng put it in *The Melancholy of Race* – here placed at the nation's centre?[47] The African Androgynes are metaphors of the vanquished subjects who, in the spectacle of succession – as the phoenix burns – become slaves of love.[48] 'After the king vanquishes his enemies he binds them with chains of love and fidelity.'[49] *Le Ballet de Madame* expresses this love of the people for the king in a particularly vivid way: The Androgynes multiply 'his happy seed' ('multiplier en nous son heureuse semence'), swarm about him like bees ('à l'entour de leur ruche mielleuse'), watch him like sentinels, and spread his seed with their hands ('Que sans cesse nos mains s'en iront emplissant').[50] Mitchell Greenberg points out 'the image of "monarchy" is one in which the political and the sexual are inextricably intertwined'.[51] In a more contemporary context Jacqueline Rose asserts: 'how an institution defines its limits, or even constitutes itself as an institution, is under-pinned by a realm in which sexual fantasy is at play'.[52]

When Greenberg says that divine right monarchy is 'a universe in which the devolution of power from male to male is mediated through the sacrifice of patriarchy's other, of the other Woman, of the feminine that must be eliminated', he underlines that the Hermaphrodite, by virtue of its presumed ability to self-reproduce, signifies male identity as a self-enclosed ontological category. The burden of any representation of the absolute king, as Greenberg shows, is the portrayal of his 'integrity of being', which is inseparable from the 'desire' of absolutism itself.[53] In this early ballet, however, integrity of being is both asserted and compromised by a *mise en scène* whose symbolic intent is self-refuting. Integrity and closure open out onto exceptionality. As Agamben shows, exceptionality is unspeakable and exists in a zone of indistinction. The remnant or fragment – a scene saturated with phantasm, melancholy, incest, and sexual imbroglio – is an allegory of indistinction. Allegory counteracts symbol.

OSIRIS AND ISIS

Elie Garel's commentary attempts to control the ballet's political-sexual disorder by distinguishing between androgyny's 'literal' interpretation and its deeper ('celestial') meaning. He adds another allegorical layer to the Hermaphrodite's ambiguities, that of the Egyptian deities Osiris and Isis.

Osiris is the murdered Egyptian king whose body was dismembered and scattered throughout Egypt. Isis was Osiris' consort (and also his sister) who must reassemble Osiris's dismembered body. Egyptologist Tom Hare explains that the role of Isis 'is to search out and collect the pieces of Osiris's body and, more important still, to resuscitate him and conceive of him a child'.[54] Drawing on this narrative, *Les Oracles François* interprets the 'Ballet des Androgynes' in a way that focuses upon the people's androgyny.

C'est donc le puissant effect de ce saint Eros moteur des ames entierement Françoises que le Sieur Durand nous monstre en cette figure, lequel agist d'une si violente façon en elles, soit qu'il les tire vers nostre grand Osiris, ou vers nostre cher Isis, que tous autres desirs forclos elles ne respirent que le seul amour de leurs Majestés, és douces delices duquel venant à se plonger du tout, elles deviennent veritablement Androgynes. Femelles, en conservant voeux sur voeux, et souhaits sur souhaits de voir un perpetuel accroissement de leur grandeur royale. Masles en produisant les fertiles effets de si legitimes desirs, avec l'accomplissement de voeux si dignes d'une affection vraiment Françoise.[55]

[Sieur Durand shows us the powerful effect of this saintly Eros, engine of entirely French souls in this figure [the Hermaphrodite], which acts so violently on those souls [the Androgynes], that it draws them either toward our great Osiris, or toward our cherished Isis, so that all other desires set aside, the souls only breathe the love of their Majesties, in the sweet enjoyment of whom they are entirely plunged that they truly become Androgynes. As such they are female in preserving wish upon wish to see the perpetual increase of their royal grandeur. And they are male in producing the fertile effects of such legitimate desires, through the accomplishment of such wishes worthy of truly French affection].

'Leurs Majestez' in this text are in the most visual sense Elizabeth and Louis in *Le Ballet de Madame* – they are, like Isis and Osiris, sister and brother – but 'Their Majesties' are also father and son (the dismembered and the remembered) whose combination in one body assures the continuity of monarchy. It is implied that the deceased father, like the dismembered Osiris, must inseminate Isis/Louis.[56] Garel writes that the Androgynes – a figure of the feminised and racialised people – are moved by a 'saintly eroticism' ('ce saint Eros moteur des âmes'), and thus 'violently' drawn ('d'une si violente façon') by turns to Osiris (the dead king) and to Isis (his re-membering and re-engendering consort). 'La France et son peuple fidele' are moved to desire both sister and brother, son and father. Here again, there is a gendering of memorialisation and rebirth, represented by these eroticised and racialised beings that are excluded from power by absorption into the incestuous couples.[57] In this way, the female sex of the Hermaphrodite is disavowed, displaced onto the people, and transferred, to recall Marin's terms, from the principle of reason of state to its project.

CONCLUSION

By eluding sex assignment in *Le Ballet de Madame* the king also eludes the juridical construction of the male subject on stage. The Hermaphrodite is as much a being of non-closure as an exemplar of the impossible integrity of male identity itself as posited by absolutism. Therefore, I propose in conclusion that the phantasm of the king's absolutist identity (political and sexual) is best accounted for by the state of exception.

Carl Schmitt, gave the following definition of political sovereignty: 'Sovereign is he who decides on the exception'.[58] 'The exception,' continued Schmitt, 'is that which cannot be subsumed; it defies general codification, but it simultaneously reveals a specifically juristic element – the decision in absolute purity.'[59] Here it is not sufficient to say that the dancing sovereign *decides* on the exception. We should rather say: the sovereign *embodies* the exception, *becomes* the exception for all to see. As such he is situated outside the symbolic order of sexually determined identity, patriarchal normativity, and, to a certain degree, beyond the precincts of classical iconography.[60]

When engraved on a medal the hermaphrodite image may well betoken the permanence of monarchy. But when the king dances the Hermaprodite, he introduces time and melancholy into the symbolism of power; he intimates bodily fragmentation and surplus with his real, because visibly present, presence. The difference between the authority of classical iconography (emblem) and the king's historical performance (theatricality) can be summed up in the difference between the sun and flame, light and heat, command and seduction, mourning and melancholy. The power of dance to dilate images in time and space removes them from the performativity of the symbolic register and places them between the real and the imaginary, in the realm of phantasm, which is also the realm of the theatrical. The performativity of dance, in other terms, is not exclusively in the service of the symbolic register, but exceeds the limits of its iconographic sources. In this sense, each gesture, each step, is an exception to the one that precedes it. Time is the privileged medium through which exceptionality is given to our senses.

To avoid the incarnation model of the body politic/body natural binary we come upon the body natural in its theatrical integrity as an *incorporating* body, and therefore as a body whose identity cannot be definitively fixed. Far from being purely surface, it is multi*pli*citous, a word that in French as well as in English contains the French term for fold: *pli*. *Le Ballet de Madame* counters the 'closure of representation', identified by Timothy Murray as the 'mimetic legacy of patriarchal absolutism'.[61] But it does so proleptically, at the dawn of that mimetic tradition. I would characterise Baroquist performance – early modern or postmodern —as performance resistant to the absolutist mimetic legacy.

In its argument for the importance of time and loss in embodied concepts of power *The Origin of German Tragic Drama* is a seminal text of baroquist modernity. Benjamin proposed allegory as an antidote to more than just the symbol in the 'Epistemo-Critical Prologue', the first chapter of *The Origin of German Tragic Drama*. Allegory, in its particular functioning within *Trauerspiel*, was an antidote to the representation of political power as a mythical force.[62] Schmitt's concept of the state of exception would seem to preempt allegory, and thus find a way to posit fascism's inevitability. For the state of exception, like allegory, is a time-based concept in which law and life become indistinct. The state of exception is, in this sense, an alternative to allegory in that power harnesses time without relinquishing its own inevitability. The point here, however, is that both allegory and the exception require a body natural to perform politics despite the fact that the collocation of the words 'body' and 'politic' usually suggests an out-of-body experience.

NOTES

1. This article develops some material discussed in my 'The King Cross-Dressed: Power and Force in Royal Ballets', published in *From the Royal to the Republican Body: Incorporating the Political in Seventeenth- and Eighteenth-Century France*, edited by Sara Melzer and Kate Norberg (Berkeley and Los Angeles: University of California Press, 1998), 64–84. Earlier drafts were read at the Maison Française, New York University (25 January 2005), 'Structures of Feeling in the Seventeenth Century', at the Clark Center, UCLA (4 June 2005), and the Maska Seminar, Cankarjev Dom, Ljubljana, Slovenia (19 February 2007).
2. Louis XIII was born 27 September 1601. The libretto was published as *Description du Ballet de Madame, soeur aisnée du Roy* (Lyon: 1615) and is held at the Bibliothèque Nationale, Paris: Yf. 973. A variant version is held at the Bibliothèque de l'Arsenal, Paris: Ra3 60.
3. This article is part of a larger project on *baroquist modernities*, by which I understand the intellectual and artistic phenomenon of recourse to the seventeenth century for contemporary reflection on language, politics and aesthetics. I have referred elsewhere to the phenomenon of reading back in time to read ahead as figural inversion. See my 'Figural Inversions of Louis XIV's Dancing Body', in *Acting on the Past: Historical Performance Across the Disciplines*, edited by Mark Franko and Annette Richards (Middletown: Wesleyan University Press, 2000): 35–51.
4. I shall also refer to the work of Ernst Kantorowicz, Louis Marin, and Georgio Agamben.
5. 'The fragment, or the remnant,' wrote Benjamin, 'is, in fact, the finest material in baroque creation.' Walter Benjamin, *The Origin of German Tragic Drama*, translated by. John Osborne (London: Verso, 1977), 178.
6. For an overview of dance's investments in the political, see Mark Franko, 'Dance and the Political: States of Exception', in *Dance Research Journal* 38/1 and 2 (Summer/Winter 2006): 3–18.

7. Ernst H. Kantorowicz, *The King's Two Bodies: a Study in Medieval Political Theology* (Princeton: Princeton University Press, 1957). This work serves as reference point even for the analysis of Ronald Reagan's body. See Brian Massumi and Kenneth Dean, 'Postmortem on the Presidential Body, or Where the Rest of Him Went', in *Body Politics. Disease, Desire, and the Family*, edited by Michael Ryan and Avery Gordon (Boulder: Westview Press, 1994), 155–74.

8. A propos of Céline's fiction Julia Kristeva calls the corpse 'the other that I am and will never reach, the horror with which I communicate no more than with the other sex during pleasure, but which dwells in me, spends me, and carries me to the point where my identity is turned into something undecidable'. Julia Kristeva, *Powers of Horror. As Essay on Abjection* translated by Leon S. Roudiez (New York: Columbia University Press, 1982), 150.

9. Ralph E. Giesey, *The Royal Funeral Ceremony in Renaissance France* (Geneva: Droz, 1960).

10. See Georgio Agamben, *Homo Sacer: Sovereign Power and Bare Life*, translated by Daniel Heller-Roazen (Stanford: Stanford University Press, 1998), especially the chapter 'Sovereign Body and Sacred Body', 91–103. Agamben neglects to observe, however, that Kantorowicz docs perceive the confusion of law and life in seventeenth-century French monarchy: '[France] eventually interpreted the absolutist rulership in such a fashion that the distinctions between personal and supra-personal aspects were blurred or even eliminated.' Kantorowicz, *The King's Two Bodies*, 446. Further pages references to *Homo Sacer* are in parentheses in the text.

11. Carl Schmitt, *Political Theology: Four Chapters in the Concept of Sovereignty*, translated by George Schwab (Cambridge: the MIT Press, 1985), 13.

12. Agamben, *Homo Sacer*, 37.

13. See Gilles Deleuze, *The Fold. Leibniz and the Baroque*. Translated by Tom Conley (Minneapolis and London: University of Minnesota Press, 1993).

14. McGowan identifies *Le Ballet de Madame* as the first French court ballet to do away with narrative entirely, and thus to valorise the spectacular production values of décor as integrated with dancing. See also McGowan's discussion of critiques by Père Menestrier of *Le Ballet de Madame* in her *L'Art du ballet de cour en France (1581–1643)* (Paris: CNRS, 1963), 89 and 95.

15. *La Continuation du Mercure François, ou, la Suitte de l'histoire de l'Auguste Regence de la Royne Marie de Medicis, sous son fils le Tres-Chretien Roy de France et de Navarre, Louis XIII*, vol. 4 (Paris: Etienne Richer, 1617), 9–23.

16. Elie Garel, *Les Oracles francois, ou explication allegorique du Balet de madame, soeur aisnee du roy* (Paris: P. Chevalier, 1615), Bibliothèque de l'Arsenal, Paris: Ra3 61, in-12. Paul Lacroix republished parts of the libretto extracted from *Les Oracles francois*. See 'Explication Allégorique du Balet de Madame', in *Ballets et mascarades de cour de Henri III à Louis XIV (1581-1652)* (Geneva: Slatkine, 1968), 2: 63–89.

17. See Margaret M. McGowan, *L'Art du ballet de cour en France*, 85–99.

18. *La Continuation du Mercure François*, vol. 4, 23 (my translation).

19. Kantorowicz, *The King's Two Bodies*, 390.

20. Sarah Hanley, 'The Monarchic State: Marital Governance and Male Right', in *Politics, Ideology, and the Law in Early Modern Europe*, edited by Adrianna E. Bakos (Rochester: University of Rochester Press, 1994), 110.

21. See 'Introduction the 1968 Edition' (Appendix I), in Norbert Elias, *The Civilizing Process. The History of Manners*, translated by Edmund Jephcott (New York: Urizen Books, 1998), 245–52. Perry Anderson points out that absolute monarchy for Marx and Engels was 'a political balancing-mechanism between nobility and bougeoisie'. Perry Anderson, *Lineages of the Absolutist State* (London: New Left Books, 1974), 16.

22. Dorinda Outram, *The Body and the French Revolution. Sex, Class and Political Culture* (New Haven and London: Yale University Press, 1989), 49.

23. Patrick Graille, *Les hermaphrodites aux XVIIe et XVIIIe siècles* (Paris: Les Belles Lettres, 2001), 114.

24. See Lorraine Daston and Katharine Park, 'The Hermaphrodite and the Orders of Nature', in *Premodern sexualities*, edited by Louise Fradenburg and Carla Freccero (New

York: Routledge, 1996), 118.

25. Kathleen Perry Long, 'Hermaphrodites Newly Discovered: the Cultural Monsters of Sixteenth-Century France', in *Monster Theory: Reading Culture* edited by Jeffrey Jerome Cohen (Minneapolis and London: University of Minnesota Press, 1996), 183–201.

26. '... [L]es deux principales marques de nos Rois, l'une qu'ils soient masles, l'autre qu'ils soient nobles: les nobles ne travaillent point: les masles ne filent point. Jamais le royaume ne tombe en quenoüille ...' ['[T]he two principle marks of our Kings [are] one, that they be male, and the other that they be noble. Nobles do not work, and males do not weave. Never should the realm go to the distaff side ...'. Pierre Dupuy, *Commentaires sur l'ordonnance de la majorité des rois*. This undated work contains an argument for majority at thirteen years, which makes it possibly contemporaneous with the *Ballet de Madame*.

27. See Julia Kristeva, *Powers of Horror* and Christine Buci-Glucksmann, *Baroque Reason. The Aesthetics of Modernity*, translated by Patrick Camiller (London: Sage Publications, 1994).

28. Ann Rosalind Jones and Peter Stallybrass, 'Fetishizing Gender: Constructing the Hermaphrodite in Renaissance Europe', in *Body Guards. The Cultural Politics of Gender Ambiguity* edited by Julia Epstein and Kristina Straub (New York and London: Routledge, 1991), 204. See also, Laura Levine, *Men in women's clothing: anti-theatricality and effeminization, 1579–1642* (Cambridge and New York: Cambridge University Press, 1994).

29. Louis Marin, *Portrait of the King*, translated by Martha M. Houle (Minneapolis: University of Minnesota Press, 1988), 193–4. Marin studies these magical effects through the role attributed to vision in narrative accounts of seventeenth-century French fête. This includes accounts of festivals in the writing of Félibien. See especially 'The Magician King, or the Prince's Fête', in *Portrait of the King*, 193–205.

30. See Jean Laplanche and J.-B. Pontalis, *The Language of Psychoanalysis*, translated by Donald Nicholson-Smith (London: the Hogarth Press, 1973), 314–19.

31. Michel Foucault, 'Theatrum Philosophicum', in *Mimesis, Masochism and Mime. The Politics of Theatricality in Contemporary French Thought*, edited by Timothy Murray (Ann Arbor: University of Michigan Press, 1997), 219.

32. Mitchell Greenberg emphasises 'the fantasy/image of the never-there king's body' in his discussion of how the phantasm is transmitted in literature of the period. When the king's body itself participates in the performance of these phantasms of state, I would argue that more anxiety is generated around its contradictions. See his *Baroque Bodies. Psychoanalysis and the Culture of French Absolutism* (Ithaca and London: Cornell University Press, 2001), 20.

33. See Sigmund Freud, 'Mourning and Melancholy', in *Collected Papers*, vol. IV: 159. See also Freud, 'The Ego and the Super Ego'. In *The Ego and the Id*, translated by Joan Rivière (New York: W.W. Norton & Co. 1960). See also the pages on 'Freud and the Melancholy of Gender', in Judith Butler, *Gender Trouble. Feminism and the Subversion of Identity* (London and New York: Routledge, 1990), 57–72.

34. 'His normally invisible body politic was on this occasion visibly displayed by the effigy in its pompous regalia: a *persona ficta* – the effigy – impersonating a *persona ficta* – the *Dignitas*.' Kantorowicz, *The King's Two Bodies*, 421.

35. Giesey, *The Royal Funeral Ceremony*, 179.

36. Ibid., 152. Among other things, the effigy is presented with ritual meals.

37. Ibid., 173. Giesey also refers to this as 'the fiction of a post-mortem sovereignty' (145).

38. For a full account of this ceremony, see Sarah Hanley, 'The Dynastic Monarchy in French Constitutional Ideology: the Inaugural Lit de Justice Assembly of 1610', in *The Lit de Justice of the Kings of France: Constitutional Ideology in Legend, Ritual, and Discourse* (Princeton: Princeton University Press, 1983), 231–53.

39. Giesey, op. cit., 189.

40. Ibid., 190.

41. Louis XIII is considered to be the first absolutist French monarch. See J. Cornette, *L'affirmation de l'état absolu* (Paris: Hachette, 1993). Hanley interprets the significance of this accession as the blunting of 'the juristic focus on office' in favor of 'a dynastic focus on blood lineage' Hanley, *The Lit de Justice*, 248. 'Discussion of the French Law of Succession was shifted in this manner from juristic to dynastic grounds, providing a rationale which legitimized the novel inaugural *Lit de Justice* assembly and a new constitutional ideology'

(ibid., p. 249).

42. See Jacobi Facciolati, *Totius Latinitas Lexicon* (1771) and Freund, *Grand Dictionnaire de la Langue Latine*.

43. Lacroix, *Ballets et mascarades de cour*, vol. 2, 83.

44. Sarah Hanley has written of 'autogenetic male generative acts' extended to the king and to the kingdom. See Sarah Hanley, 'The Monarchic State: Marital Governance and Male Right', in *Politics, Ideology, and the Law in Early Modern Europe*, edited by Adrianna E. Bakos (Rochester: University of Rochester Press, 1994), 111–12.

45. Cited in Giesey, op. cit.

46. 'Feu d'artifice', dans *L'Entrée triomphante de leurs Majestez Louis XIV Roy de France et de Navarre et Marie-Therese d'Autriche son epouse dans la ville de Paris* (Paris: 1662): 4. Bibliothèque de l'Arsenal: Ra4 306.

47. Anne Anlin Cheng, *The Melancholy of Race* (New York: Oxford University Press, 2000), 10.

48. The libretto of *Le Ballet de Madame* tells us that the Androgynes 'nourish this torch in their heart' ('Partant, continuons, celestes Androgynes, A nourrir ce Brandon tousjours dans nos poitrines'). Lacroix, *Ballets et mascarades de cour*, 83.

49. 'Aprez que le Roy a vaincu ses ennemis,' concludes the description of the entry, 'il les attache avec des chaines d'amour et de fidelité.' *L'Entrée triomphante*. The text adds: 'Le Roy est vrayment un Amour en apparence, et un Hercule en effect' ('The King is really a cupid in appearance and a Hercules in reality'). Ibid., 117.

50. Lacroix, *Ballets et mascarades de cour*, vol. 2, 82–3.

51. Mitchell Greenberg, *Canonical States, Canonical Stages. Oedipus, Othering, and Seventeenth-Century Drama* (Minneapolis: the University of Minnesota Press, 1994), 44.

52. Jacqueline Rose, *Sexuality in the Field of Vision* (London: Verso, 1986), 4.

53. The very consciousness that no boundary is impermeable drives absolutism even more ruthlessly toward 'a desire for a unity of being' – which is pertinently the unity of sexual identity (Greenberg, *Canonical States, Canonical Stages*, xxix). For Greenberg, in the seventeenth century, 'both the body and the state are cerned, being forced, as Foucault would have it, into a new model/mold of closure, into the illusion of impermeable "difference", into discrete, be it national or personal, identities' (4). As Greenberg indicates, Michel Foucault has analysed the question of subjectivity as it relates both to power and to the construct 'sexuality'. The first book of his trilogy on the history of sexuality devotes considerable attention to the question of sovereignty and how to treat the sovereign subject in the analysis of power. See Michel Foucault, *The History of Sexuality: An Introduction*, translated by Robert Hurley (New York: Vintage Books, 1990).

54. Tom Hare, *ReMembering Osiris: number, gender, and the word in ancient Egyptian representational systems* (Stanford: Stanford University Press, 1999), 122.

55. Garel, *Les Oracles françois*, 138–9.

56. Hanley has posited a 'biogenetic seminal theory of authority' for French monarchy according to which 'although a woman reproduces, she does not seminally create'. In her view, a woman could not accede to the throne of France because she might produce a successor of foreign origin. This theory replaces the discredited Salic Law prohibiting women from acceding to the throne of France, and cited in the past as the juridical basis for the patrilinearity of French monarchy. See *Dictionnaire de l'Ancien Régime: royaume de France, XVIe–XVIIIe siècle* (Paris: Presses Universitaires de France, 1996), 752–3. The Salic Law has been called a political myth in the service of legitimation. See Elie Barnavi, 'Mythes et réalité historique: le cas de la loi salique', in *Histoire économie et société* 3 (1984), 323–37, and Sarah Hanley, 'Identity Politics and Rulership in France: Female Political Place and the Fraudulent Salic Law in Christine de Pizan and Jean de Montreuil', in *Changing Identities in Early Modern France* edited by Michael Wolfe (Durham: Duke University Press, 1997), 78–94. For a discussion of the power of women as Regents, see Fannie Cosandey, '"La blancheur de nos lys". La reine de France au Coeur de l'Etat royal', in *Revue d'histoire moderne et contemporaine* 44/3 (July–September 1997), 387–403.

57. For a discussion of the incorporation of slaves into the French body politic in the seventeenth century and beyond, see Joseph R. Roach, 'Body of Law: the Sun King and the Code Noir', in *From the Royal to the Republican Body*, 113–30.

58. Schmitt, *Political Theology*, 5.
59. Ibid., 13. More recently, Georgio Agamben has argued against Schmitt that a state of exception can only be linked to the utter suspension of the law in the most sinister sense. Under the state of exception the juridical order ceases to regulate social relations: it represents a serious jeopardising of the relation of law to the symbolic order. See Georgio Agamben, *State of Exception*, translated by Kevin Attell (Chicago and London: the University of Chicago Press, 2005).
60. This important point is supported by McGowan's observation that the ballet substitutes spectacle for the literary sources in the interpretation of allegorical meaning: '[L]e spectacle se substitue à la fable littéraire ou mythologique comme base de l'allégorie'. *L'Art du ballet de cour en France*, 99. Susan Foster has argued that narrative in ballet assured the ego-logical closure of the subject from the eighteenth to the twentieth century. See her *Choreography and Narrative: Ballet's Staging of Story and Desire* (Bloomington: Indiana University Press, 1998). Spectacle, although it has been much maligned by performance studies in comparison to ritual, might be rehabilitated as a baroquist mode of continuing value for its anti-narrative qualities.
61. Timothy Murray, *Mimesis, Masochism and Mime*, 9.
62. The distinction between allegory and symbol was taken up in the 1980s when the notion of allegory came back into vogue as a form of postmodern aesthetics. What was crucially missed in these discussions was the distinction between allegory and myth that gives the neo-baroque, in my view, its political rationale. See Craig Owens, 'The Allegorical Impulse: Toward a Theory of Postmodernism', *October* 12 (Spring 1980), 67–86.

Dancing Towards Death: Masques and Entertainments in London and Florence as precedents for Thomas Middleton's *Women Beware Women*

MARGARET SHEWRING AND J. R. MULRYNE

Thomas Middleton's tragedy Women Beware Women *(c.1613–21) includes in its fifth act a masque during which the play's miscreants are severally killed and its corrupt society collapses. The masque's debt to Ben Jonson's* Hymenaei *is discussed, together with its possible recollection of Florentine entertainments, including those staged in 1586 for the wedding of Cesare d' Este with Virginia de' Medici. The play is based on fact, centring on the seduction of Bianca Cappello and her marriage with the Grand Duke Francesco de' Medici. Middleton makes considerable efforts to provide an 'authentic' Florentine setting for his play including, it is suggested, recalling the celebrated series of Medici wedding entertainments and touching on the fascination of an early seventeenth-century elite society with Florentine culture.*

Thomas Middleton's remarkable tragedy, *Women Beware Women*, has been dated by most commentators to 1620–1, but was possibly first written some years earlier, in, it may be, 1613–14.[1] The play portrays a failed society, a veritable dystopia, where personal, social and political relations are characterised by marital deception, rape and murder, with, in the notorious concluding masque, a full harvest of technicolour occurrences, including the use as weapons of offence of poisoned smoke, deadly Cupids and a shower of burning gold. Our aim in this article is to relate Middleton's play to English and Florentine dance forms, specifically court masques and entertainments, and in so doing to complement and extend current scholarship.

The play's narrative is based on fact, suitably dressed and managed to serve the needs of a five-act drama, but hewing surprisingly close nonetheless to reports of 1570s and 1580s Florence as these were known in London some forty or fifty years later. Events surrounding the marriage and death of Bianca Cappello, second wife of Francesco de' Medici, Grand Duke of Tuscany (1541–87), had from the outset been associated with scandal. The chronicler and gossip writer Celio Malespini's *Ducento Novelle* (Venice, 1609) tells the story of the aristocratic Bianca's elopement and marriage with the bank employee Pietro Buonaventura, a Florentine working in Venice for the Salviati bank, her notorious affair and eventual wedding with Francesco, and the death of the errant pair within hours of each other at the ducal villa of Poggio a Caiano. Their deaths occasioned immediate and lasting speculations of foul play on the part of Francesco's brother and successor, Ferdinand, the Cardinal in *Women Beware Women*. Distribution of manuscript accounts across Europe, together with word of mouth, ensured the tale became common gossip, festering in the minds of the curious until at least the eighteenth century.[2] Middleton's achievement, we shall argue, is to embed his version of the Bianca story in a seemingly actual Florence, drawing for authentic effect, alongside other devices, on entertainments staged for Medici weddings during the relevant period. Dance and dance-related theatre forms provide the playwright, we argue, with one means of anchoring the play's chief concerns in a strongly-imagined Florence.

Masques can be considered the epitome of elite social dance in the first half of the seventeenth century, rooted in considerable measure in Tudor masques and disguisings but receiving a marked impetus from the new style of courtly masque commissioned by Queen Anne. Written and designed most often by Ben Jonson and Inigo Jones, these masques were greatly influenced by continental European practice, especially that of the Italian city states, notably Florence.[3] 'The chief element of this form of entertainment had always been dancing', Andrew J. Sabol writes, boldly elevating dance above either 'fable', Ben Jonson's territory, or design, Inigo Jones's.[4] Neither Jonson nor Jones might be expected to agree, but the social element of the masque, whether during included dances or in the 'revels' which lengthily climaxed the show – with noble spectators in the audience 'taken out' by their masquing social equals – must have seemed to the participants a major element, perhaps *the* major element, of the evening. Given the extensive rehearsals that preceded the actual occasion, during which spectacle, music and movement were (ideally) brought together, and given the imposing presence among the onlookers of royalty, nobility and foreign ambassadors, the potential of masques for high level social bonding, and on more than one occasion its contrary – disharmony and self-aggrandisement – must be counted, despite masques' relatively infrequent occurrence, among potential contributions to elite social order or its opposite. Behind each occasion, reinforced by the newly minted text, loomed the familiar iconography of dancing which shadowed, as Sabol puts it, 'an ideal world in which right reason, virtuous fame, and altruistic love triumph over the mean and paltry concerns of a nether world'.[5] When Middleton introduced a masque as the culmination of his tragedy he was drawing, at two removes, on embedded associations in the minds of his audience, including the minds of those, whether at the Globe, the Blackfriars or elsewhere, who had never attended a court masque, but merely heard about these high-profile occasions, and regarded them as inherently indicative of generic court culture. A masque which inverts the usual values of the form takes on an enhanced force as an adverse critique of the prevailing social order.[6]

It is not difficult to demonstrate the allusiveness of *Women Beware Women* to Ben Jonson's and Inigo Jones's *Hymenaei*, the elaborate masque staged to celebrate the 1606 nuptials of Frances Howard and Robert Devereux.

Middleton's *Masque of Juno*, as we may name the catastrophic masque of the play's fifth act, echoes its Jonsonian precedent in personnel – Juno and Hymen – in the prominence assumed by Juno, in Middleton's implicit references to Jonson's employment and explanation, in text and notes, of the iconology of marriage, and in his even more clearly marked allusions to certain memorable staging devices. Livia's 'descent' as Juno in *Women Beware Women*, though a characteristic episode, as we shall see, in the stage practice of the Florentine entertainments, and therefore unoriginal here, bears a distinct resemblance to Jonson's handling of the Juno figure in *Hymenaei*. Visual reminiscence during a performance of Middleton's play, where 'LIVIA *descends like Juno*' (5.2.97 s.d.),[7] recalls Juno 'in the top' (i.e. in an elevated position on stage), 'sitting in a Throne, supported by two beautifull Peacockes' in the Jonson masque. There are other visual reminiscences, or potential reminiscences, for audiences viewing *The Masque of Juno*. Juno's altar, the main stage-property in Middleton (see 5.2.72.s.d.) harks back to the altar inscribed to Juno at *Hymenaei* lines 32–7. The spectacular action performed by Middleton's goddess, '*Throws flaming gold upon Isabella, who falls dead*' (5.2.117 s.d.), as described in a contemporary note in the Yale University copy of the play, and her reference to Jove's 'burning treasure' (5.2.118), sit well with the relevant stage direction in Jonson: '*Above her [i.e. Juno] the region of fire … and Jupiter [i.e. Jove] standing in the top, figuring the heaven, brandishing his thunder*'. The further amplification of the direction, 'Juno in a glorious throne of gold, circled with comets and fiery meteors' (lines 593–4), confirms the prominence of the effect. It looks from these allusions, and other hints, that Middleton had Jonson's masque very much in mind as he composed his own, thereby allowing informed audience members to recall the earlier show and its occasion.

Hymenaei, it could be argued, offers the most comprehensive embodiment of ideal marriage on the English stage, its performance text backed by learned and extensive classical authority. Allusion to *Hymenaei* provided Middleton, therefore, with an effective shorthand for those often buried but influential conceptions in the Jacobean mind of the social and cultural meanings of marriage. *Hymenaei* came with its own freight of associations, however, for the marriage it celebrated in 1606, between Frances Howard and Robert Devereux, had become by 1613–14 an occasion of rumour and scandal as the married pair sought annulment on the grounds of the groom's sexual incapacity. By two years later, after Frances had married the current royal favourite Robert Carr, salacious gossip turned to still darker speculation as the pair were tried for complicity in the murder of Sir Thomas Overbury, a former associate, and consigned to the Tower. Recollection of these events through reference to *Hymenaei* must have coloured response to *The Masque of Juno*, so reinforcing an informed audience's sense of the social dysfunction the play addresses.[8]

Women Beware Women is set in Florence and thus responds to a distinct strand in the prevailing culture of the early years of the seventeenth century. It is usual in current commentary to explain foreign settings in Jacobean plays as motivated by an author's wary avoidance of home-grown surveillance and censorship – conveniently displacing criticism of James's court on to regimes abroad. There is truth in this. But the care with which Middleton has researched his Florentine sources, appearing to have consulted both printed and manuscript material, taken together with the play's repeated allusions to Florentine locations and practices, suggests a motivation that goes beyond providing a superficial gloss of foreignness. The play becomes a Florence-London hybrid, not only referring to members of the Medici family – by no means out of living memory in London – but employing seemingly incidental details to confirm the Florentine connection. To take a single example, Bianca's seduction takes place in a palazzo distinguished by the presence of a nobleman's art collection (2.2.271–8). Elite culture in James's London was defining itself at this time by the possession of Italian art-works (Venetian and Florentine chiefly), with the active participation of leading nobles including the Earl of Arundel, the royal favourite Buckingham and, intriguingly, Robert Carr, seen by A. R. Braunmuller as 'avant-garde' in his tastes as a collector.[9] At Carr's death, among the paintings in his possession were depictions of Samson and Delilah, Venus and Cupid, Susanna and the Elders (possibly Tintoretto's *Susanna Bathing* with its full-scale naked Susanna), Bacchus, Ceres and Venus, and Venus and Adonis, all likely to have included invitingly naked figures. Bianca is shown 'naked pictures' 'A bit to stay the appetite' in preparation for the Duke's amorous attentions (2.2.401–4). This is not to suggest that Middleton has Carr directly in mind, merely that the Florence of the play may be expected to evoke for its audience the Italy- and Florence-conscious elite society of London.[10]

More central to the play's narrative, and our purposes, *The Masque of Juno* recollects for those aware of them the lavish series of Medici festival entertainments which brought Florence to the attention of Europe and which provided the groundwork for the Jacobean court masque. Florentine entertainments had their place in courtly and creative minds in England in the early years of the century, as the English played catch-up with more sophisticated European regimes.[11] Entertainments for Francesco's first marriage, to take a relevant example, seem to have supplied the inspiration for ideas incorporated in *The Haddington Masque* (1608).[12] Roy Strong has highlighted the specific interest of Prince Henry's court in the Florentine entertainments, noting that Henry commissioned his companion and member of his court John Harington to attend the celebrations in Florence in November 1608 for the marriage of the Grand Duke's son Cosimo to the archduchess Maria Maddalena, ordering him to report back with full descriptions.[13] Harington's letters from Florence are unfortunately lost, but the episode shows how senior royalty, even at Henry's tender age, were eager to learn the ways of Florentine shows. The presence in Henry's court of Constantino de' Servi, a Florentine originally in the service of Grand Duke Francesco in the 1570s, no doubt strengthened London curiosity about Francesco and the Florentine entertainments.[14] Middleton's interest in these shows seems likely to have been sparked, in *Women Beware Women*, by his almost documentary attention to the history of Francesco and Bianca – which he would have wished to flesh out authentically – and his consequent investigation, as it appears, of possible source-texts for *The Masque of Juno* among the Medici entertainments.

It is inviting, as the most obvious source, to link *The Masque of Juno* with the entertainments for Francesco's marriage with Bianca in Florence in October 1579. The occasion was a lavish one, perhaps in compensation for Bianca's lacking ducal or royal blood, and to compensate also for the awkward circumstance that Bianca's earlier, adulterous, relationship with Francesco was well-known and widely deplored. The Palazzo Vecchio was called into service as were various outdoor locations, but the most spectacular event took place at the Palazzo Pitti, the *cortile* of which was covered over for the occasion by a huge suspended cloth and brilliantly lit. Noble visitors from Vicenza, Verona and Padua were present, along with Bianca's father, various relatives, and official ambassadors from Venice. Middleton might well have been intrigued by the political opportunism of the occasion when 'I Clarissimi Ambasciatori fatta vna bella, e numerosa orazione ripiena di nobilissimi concetti', in the course of which 'tutti insieme pronunziauano la nuoua Gran Duchessa vera, & vnica figliuola dello loro Republica, e di San Marco'.[15] Years earlier, the Venetian Council of Ten (10 December 1563) had pronounced Bianca and her first husband Pietro Buonaventura undesirable outlaws and placed a price on their heads. Bianca's elevation to high rank and riches evidently made a difference to Venetian perception. The author of the *descrizione* of the occasion, Raffaelo Gualterotti, is hugely impressed by the brilliant lighting of the theatre space, repeatedly mentioned, and by the attentiveness of the spectators: 'Era il luminoso, e pomposo teatro ripiena di vn mirabile silenzio' (p. 12), a phenomenon perhaps not invariably or even usually experienced at Florentine festivals.[16] The entertainment's fable is of a familiar romance-based kind, with a 'donzella isconsolata' rescued by Apollo, a splendid five-headed fire-breathing dragon, a judgment of Paris (Bianca is of course awarded the apple), an appearance by Venus and naked Cupids, and a rather daring political statement as the Lion of St Mark is displayed impaled with the arms of the house of Cappello – the last in support of the proposition that the women of Venice (especially Bianca) are the most beautiful of all – sentiments which unsurprisingly Middleton's Duke reiterates in Act 3 scene 3 (22–8 and 77–8). One episode only, however, might be thought to have furnished a hint for Middleton, when two warriors (*Guerrieri*) ask Venus to decide between them (p. 29), thus providing a possible source for the contest between two lovers which Juno is asked to arbitrate in Middleton (5.2.34–44). Otherwise, the marriage ceremonies for Francesco and Bianca, assuming Middleton had access to them, might have impressed him as theatrically notable, but not specifically fruitful for his own purposes.

There can be no doubt that Italian and especially Florentine festival practice influenced Middleton's writing of *The Masque of Juno*, either indirectly through the work of Jonson and Jones or, as we have grown to think, by way of direct access to printed or manuscript *descrizioni*. There are, however, few or no incontrovertible instances of straightforward verbal borrowing. Middleton wrote under the constraints of the theatrical resources available for staging his masque in a public playhouse, so that as he wrote his main consideration must have been finding ways of presenting the sequence of punishments meted out to the play's various miscreants. Nevertheless, the play's masque is reminiscent of several Medici wedding festivals in subject matter if not in details of expression. One tantalising if slight instance relates to the most celebrated and most widely-known of all the entertainments, in England as elsewhere, the *intermedii* interspersed between the acts of Bargagli's *La Pellegrina*, staged in 1589 for the wedding of Francesco's successor (and rumoured assassin), the Grand Duke Ferdinand, with the French princess Christine of Lorraine. The writer of one account published in Venice, perhaps for the Venetian market, thought he saw, at the outset of Intermedio 4, the car of Juno pass so lightly and swiftly through the sky, drawn by two '*animali*' (presumably, as he thought, her customary peacocks), that it was impossible to discern how it reached the midst of the heavens.[17] Only as this car disappeared, the writer reported, did the notorious Inferno erupt, described with relish by other commentators as the main subject of this *intermedio*. The Ward of *Women Beware Women* seems to envisage a kind of modest Inferno when he recalls an incendiary one-eyed devil rising out of a trapdoor during 'the last triumph' 'with a company of fireworks at's tail' (5.1.7–9). The similarity here, while intriguing, is scarcely overwhelming.

Hints of Middleton's possible knowledge of the entertainments to mark Francesco's first marriage, with Joanna of Austria in December 1565, may be uncovered.[18] The occasion of this first marriage must have been in Middleton's mind as he composed his play – Livia explicitly mentions 'the first marriage of the Duke' (4.2.203), for which, she tells us, Guardiano had prepared a 'device' (4.2.202–10). Among the *intermedii* staged between the acts of Francesco D'Ambra's *La Cofanaria* in 1565 were two involving grotesques reminiscent of the part the Ward envisages for himself in the concluding scene of *Women Beware Women*. His role of Slander will entail him sporting, he says, 'a foul fiend's head with a long contumelious tongue i' th' chaps on 't' (5.1.19–20),[19] a character mentioned again in the 'argument' of the masque as read out by the Duke (5.1.32–44). This figure of Slander consorts readily with the series of moral vices paraded through the fourth and fifth *intermedii* of the Florentine show, including Discordia, Ira and Crudelta, with, closer to Middleton, 'noiosa Gelosia' and Invidia, the latter wearing her customary posse of snakes. Vendetta, another of the emblematic figures, has a nest of vipers for a headpiece, perhaps giving rise to the Ward's allusion to his own envisaged fiend's-head costume.

However suggestive these similarities may be – there are others in other Medici wedding entertainments – the most substantial likenesses between play and printed *descrizione* come in the text attributed to Bastiano de' Rossi for the nuptials (February 1586) of Cesare d'Este, duke of Ferrara, and Virginia de' Medici, Francesco's half-sister.[20] The *intermedii*, performed between the acts of Giovanni Bardi's *L'Amico fido*, were staged in the new theatre at the Uffizi, under the direction of a top-level team of writers, artists and designers including de'

Bardi and Bernardo Buontalenti.[21] The same team worked together again on the celebrated 1589 *intermedii*. De' Rossi's description of the 1586 event is enthusiastic to the point of inviting scepticism on the reader's part: *'per la grandessa, bellezza, spesa, e artificio dell' apparato, e per la 'nuenzione e marauiglia degl' intermedi non restasse vinta da alcuna, che ... in Italia fosse recitata giammai'* (sig. A1v). But even if inflated language is routine in the *descrizioni*, there can be no question that the occasion was indeed spectacular, costly, and more integrated in theme than previous entertainments. Strong is of the opinion that if the publicity that greeted these *intermedii* had been as extensive as that for the 1589 show, the 1586 entertainment would be regarded as the seminal event of the dazzling series that followed.[22] It is not unlikely therefore, on the face of it, that Middleton, if he were seeking to research the literature of the Medici weddings, would have been acquainted with this text.

This is not the place to offer a blow-by-blow discussion of the similarities between *descrizione* and play. It will be enough to point out that the two texts share a notable range of material, in personnel (gods and morality figures), in spectacular events, and in sentiment – sentiment that is ironically inverted for the purposes of Middleton's dystopian revels. The de' Bardi text includes (fifth *intermedio*) not only a wonderfully-costumed Juno in a car drawn by peacocks (Fabritio specifically mentions Juno's 'peacocks' feathers' at 5.2.138) but also Nymphs, Cupids, Hymen, Ganymede, all of them common to Middleton. In the sixth *intermedio* there appear 'Pastori Eroi', prefiguring, it may be, the wretched Hippolito and Guardiano, costumed *'like shepherds'* for their intervention in the masque (5.2.89 s.d.), yet soon to be done to death, in full contrast with the fortunate pastors of the Florentine text. The Ward, too, would find in de' Bardi a quota of possible precedents for his acting role playing Slander: the second *intermedio* features L'Invidia, L'Ira and La Discordia, with others, though de' Bardi imagines these more often as female hags than as Ward-like impersonations – L'Invidia is 'vna bruttissima vecchia, magra e pallida', with wrinkled, pendulous female breasts (sig C4v). The Ward would find his devils, too, in the same *intermedio*. They swarm shrieking across the stage, engendering 'lo spavento, e l'orrore'. The whole city of Florence seems through the agency of the devils to be in flames, a rather more spectacular conflagration, it's true, than the 'company of fireworks' in Middleton.

Of greater interest to an interpreter are inversions that are, it's possible to suppose, conscious, on Middleton's part, of some of the more striking effects of the Florentine show. Cupids, in the company of Zephyr, Nymphs and Satyrs, Pan and Priapus, are associated in Florence (*intermedio* three), with the recovery of the previously barren countryside to a newly flourishing condition. In *Women Beware Women*, Cupids bring death. Again, one of the most spectacular visual features in Florence was the manner in which the car of Juno was sustained aloft and then disappeared, spirited on and off by unseen means: 'Questa [nugola] si sostenne sempre nell' aria, ne mai in alcun luogo posò' (sig. E4v). Middleton's Juno by contrast crash-landed, provoking Fabritio's bemused remark: 'Look, Juno's down too, / What makes she there? Her pride should keep aloft; / She was wont to scorn the earth in other shows' (5.2.135–7). A nice touch in de' Bardi is the dispersal into the streets of Florence, represented on the perspective stage with detailed realism, of the gods who descend with Hymen to bring marriage-blessings to the city's inhabitants. It is tempting to guess at Middleton's ironic satisfaction as he inverted this image – the streets of *his* Florence are occupied by greed, lust and death. As Hippolito remarks, 'Lust and forgetfulness has been amongst us, / And we are brought to nothing' (5.2.146–7). The Cardinal later concurs: 'The greatest sorrow and astonishment / That ever struck the general peace of Florence / Dwells in this hour' (198–200). Perhaps the most spectacular effect in Middleton's *Masque of Juno*, captured in the note in the Yale copy, comes when Juno '*Throws flaming gold upon Isabella, who falls dead*' (5.2.117 s.d.). Livia in her role as Juno accompanies this action with the remark, 'Now for a sign of wealth and golden days, / Bright-eyed prosperity which all couples love, / Ay, and makes love, take that – Our brother Jove / Never denies us of his burning treasure, / T'express bounty' (5.2.115–19). Is this Middleton's inversion of the Blessings ('Beni') which are showered upon Florence in the first *intermedio* of the earlier show? Spectators at that show saw Florence, given prominence by the perspective setting, blessed and revived by the bounty of the gods. Middleton's Florence-that-is-also-London is by contrast reduced to moral and political chaos.

It has not been the purpose of this article to identify specific 'sources' for *The Masque of Juno*, but rather to enquire whether Middleton's theatrical imagination may have been nourished by a study not only of Jonson's and Jones's Florentine-influenced invention of the Stuart court masque, but also of the Florentine *intermedii* associated in history with the events of his play. If the latter is the case, especially, his masque accords with the sense of location he so carefully articulates elsewhere in *Women Beware Women*, and with a more general interest in things Florentine among his immediate contemporaries. As they dance towards death, it could be claimed, Middleton's characters carry with them not only the playwright's severely moralistic judgement on the morals of his society but also his implicit report on the Florentine strain in elite contemporary culture.

NOTES

1. For a discussion of dating of the play, see J. R. Mulryne (ed.), *Women Beware Women*, the Revels Plays (Manchester: Manchester University Press, 1975), Introduction, pp. xxxii–xxxviii.
2. Ibid., for Sources, pp. xxxiii–li and 168–79.
3. For the continental European, including Florentine, influence on the physical realisation of the Stuart court masque see John Peacock, *The Stage Designs of Inigo Jones: the European Context* (Cambridge: Cambridge University Press, 1995) and Peacock, 'Ben Jonson and the Italian Festival Books', in J. R. Mulryne and Margaret Shewring (eds), *Theatre of the English and Italian Renaissance* (Houndmills and London: Macmillan, 1991, pp. 73–94. See also the magnificent volumes by Stephen Orgel and Roy Strong, *Inigo Jones: The Theatre of the Stuart Court*, 2 vols (London, Berkeley and Los Angeles: Sotheby, Parke Bernet and the University of California Press, 1973).
4. Andrew J. Sabol (ed.), *Four Hundred Songs and Dances from the Stuart Masque* (Hanover and London: University Press of New England for Brown University Press, 1978), p. 3.

5. Sabol, p. 3, fn 1.
6. For an excellent discussion of masques in plays, see Inga-Stina Ewbank, 'These Pretty Devices: A Study of Masques in Plays', in *A Book of Masques in Honour of Allardyce Nicoll* (Cambridge: Cambridge University Press, 1967), pp. 407–48.
7. References in round brackets are to J. R. Mulryne (ed.), *Women Beware Women*, The Revels Plays Student Editions (Manchester: Manchester University Press, 2007). Quotations from Ben Jonson's *Hymenaei* are taken from Stephen Orgel (ed.), *Ben Jonson, The Complete Masques* (New Haven and London: Yale University Press, 1969), pp. 75–106.
8. Writers called on to celebrate the second marriage of Frances Howard responded in ways that betrayed their self-conscious awkwardness with the assignment. Poems by Jonson and Donne are edgy and replete with evasive tactics, the anonymous *Masque of Flowers* and Campion's *Somerset Masque* are poor things, the latter panned by audiences, including the Agent of Savoy who wrote a damning critique of the masque's staging by the Florentine Constantino de' Servi. See John Orrell, 'The Agent of Savoy at the Somerset Masque', *Review of English Studies* (1977), 301–4 and David Lindley, 'Embarrassing Ben: the Masques for Frances Howard', *English Literary Renaissance* 16 (1986), 343–59. For detailed discussion of Frances's adventures, see Anne Somerset, *Unnatural Murder, Poison at the Court of James I* (London: Weidenfeld & Nicolson, 1997) and David Lindley, *The Trials of Frances Howard, Fact and Fiction at the Court of King James* (London and New York: Routledge, 1993). A. A. Bromham and Zara Bruzzi have made a strong case for Middleton's preoccupation with the Frances Howard scandals in their study *The Changeling and the Years of Crisis, 1619–1624: A Hieroglyph of Britain* (New York and London: Pinter Publishers, 1990).
9. A. R. Braunmuller, 'Robert Carr, Earl of Somerset, as Collector and Patron', in Linda Levy Peck (ed.), *The Mental World of the Jacobean Court* (Cambridge: Cambridge University Press, 1991), pp. 230–50 (p. 230).
10. Carr was, Jerry Brotton notes, 'acutely aware of the need for an art collection appropriate to his status'. He took possession in 1615 of a remarkable collection of Venetian paintings, including Titian's erotic Venus, or a studio copy of it. See Jerry Brotton, *The Sale of the Late King's Goods: Charles I and His Art Collection* (London, Basingstoke and Oxford: Pan Macmillan, 2006), p. 58. For more extended discussion of the Florentine-London crossover in the play see the Introduction to the Revels Student edition of *Women Beware Women*, esp. pp. 8–14. For the acquisition of Florentine and other works of art in seventeenth century London, see, in addition to Brotton, David Howarth, *The Earl of Arundel and his Circle* (New Haven and London: Yale University Press, 1985) and *Art and Patronage in the Caroline Courts* (Cambridge: Cambridge University Press, 1993).
11. For the proliferation of festivals in the sixteenth century see J. R. Mulryne, Helen Watanabe-O'Kelly and Margaret Shewring (eds), *Europa Triumphans: Court and Civic Festivals in Early Modern Europe*, 2 vols (Aldershot and Burlington, VT: Ashgate, 2004) and 'Expert Views' by J. R. Mulryne, Alexander Samson, David Sanchez and Helen Watanabe O'Kelly in *Renaissance Festival Books in the British Library*, www.bl.uk, on-line collection, Treasures in Full, project directors J. R. Mulryne and Margaret Shewring. For the Florentine festivals specifically see A. M. Nagler, *Theatre Festivals of the Medici: 1539–1637* (New Haven and London: Yale University Press, 1964). The influence of Florence on staging practices adopted by Inigo Jones, especially in following designs by Bernardo Buontalenti and even more so Giulio Parigi, is fully mapped in John Peacock *The Stage Designs*, who identifies the source of designs used in Jonson's and Jones's *Masque of Blackness* as work done for the first and second weddings of the play's Grand Duke Francesco.
12. John Peacock, 'Ben Jonson and the Italian Festival Books', p. 280.
13. Roy Strong, *Henry Prince of Wales and England's Lost Renaissance* (London: Thames and Hudson, 1986), p. 138.
14. Strong, *Henry Prince of Wales*, p. 92 quotes a petition from de' Servi to the secretary of the current Grand Duke in August 1611, asking to be sent copies of masque designs by Bernardo Buontalenti stemming from 'the time of the Grand Duke Francesco up to now'. For de' Servi's biography see Strong, pp. 88–105.
15. Raffaello Gualterotti, *Feste Nelle Nozze del Serenissimo Don Francesco Medici … et della Sig[nora]Bianca Cappello* (Florence, 1579), p. 7.

16. Gualterotti comments more than once on 'il silentio, che pareua cosa mirabile fra tante gente' (p. 17), a silence, he says 'che haueua in se vna tacita eloquenza' (p. 14).
17. See Anon, *Li Sontvosissimi Apparecchi, Trionfi, e Feste, Fatte Nelle Nozze della Gran Dvchessa di Fiorenza* (Venice, 1589). Giuseppe Pavoni saw, for his *descrizione*, probably correctly, a sorceress, not Juno, though perhaps he failed to report an appearance by Juno in the same *intermedio*. (For Pavoni's account, see Nagler, *Theatre Festivals*, p. 84). Middleton might have consulted the anonymous text, not Pavoni, and so have been unaware of the discrepancy. For a full discussion of the *intermedii* for the Ferdinand and Christine marriage, see James M. Saslow, *The Medici Wedding of 1589, Florentine Festival as 'Theatrum Mundi'* (New Haven and London: Yale University Press, 1996). See also Arthur R. Blumenthal, *Theater Art of the Medici* (Hanover, NH and London: University Press of New England, 1980), pp. 2–27.
18. See Domenico Mellini, attr., *Descrizione dell' Apparato della Comedia et Intermedii … Recitata in Firenze …nelle reali nozze dell' … Don Francesco Medici … e della Regina Giouanna d' Austria sua consorte* (Florence, 1566).
19. F. G. Fleay suggested that Middleton borrowed this figure from Dekker's *Troia Nova Triumphans*, and it may be so, though there are question marks over the identification. See Mulryne (ed.), *Women Beware Women*, Revels Plays edition, 1975, pp. xxxii–xxxiii.
20. Bastiano de' Rossi, *Descrizione del Magnificentiss. Apparato … nelle felicissime Nozze degl' … Signor Don Cesare D'Este e la Signora Donna Virginia Medici* (Florence, 1585 [Feb. 1586]). For staging see Strong *Art and Power, Renaissance Festivals 1450–1650* (Bury St. Edmunds: The Boydell Press 1984), pp. 134–6 and Nagler *Theatre* Festivals, ch. 5, pp. 58–69.
21. Strong, *Art and Power*, p. 134, and Nagler, *Theatre Festivals*, pp. 58–69. For expert discussion of the practical demands of staging *intermedii* see Roger Savage, 'Checklists for Philostrate', in J. R. Mulryne and Elizabeth Goldring (eds), *Court Festivals of the European Renaissance: Art, Politics and Performance* (Aldershot and Burlington, VT: Ashgate, 2002), pp. 294–307, and Roger Savage, 'The Performance and Staging of Courtly Theatre', Expert Views, the British Library website (as note 10 above).
22. Strong, *Art and Power*, p. 134.

Burlesque Ballet, a Ballad and a Banquet in Ben Jonson's *The Gypsies Metamorphos'd* (1621)

BARBARA RAVELHOFER

In summer 1621, George Villiers, then Marquess of Buckingham, invited the king and an exclusive circle of courtiers to inaugurate his newly restored countryside residence Burley-on-the-Hill in Rutland, Lincolnshire. On this occasion, he commissioned Ben Jonson with a masque, The Gypsies Metamorphos'd, *in which he himself and various friends performed as dancing, pick-pocketing and palm-reading gipsies.* The Gypsies Metamorphos'd *was a risqué piece which experimented with innovative features, some of them outrageous. In particular, Jonson and his collaborators drew upon French-style ballet and banqueting fashions which they combined with traditional English music and song. This essay explains the reason for these artistic choices.*

In summer 1621, George Villiers, then Marquess of Buckingham, invited the king and an exclusive circle of courtiers to inaugurate his newly restored countryside residence Burley-on-the-Hill in Rutland, Lincolnshire.[1] On this occasion, he commissioned Ben Jonson with a masque to entertain the visitors. At the time, Jonson was already a long-established poet and dramatist who had acquired an excellent reputation as a specialist in sumptuous courtly spectacle and ballet, which he orchestrated together with the famous architect and stage designer Inigo Jones. For Buckingham, however, Jonson prepared no high-maintenance production but a comparatively light entertainment inspired by Continental taste: *The Gypsies Metamorphos'd* was an informal event in which Buckingham himself and various friends and relatives participated as performers. Buckingham, the poet Endymion Porter, Nicholas Lanier and gentlemen of King James's bedchamber entered the stage as dancing and palm-reading gipsies.[2] Buckingham's crew told the fortunes of select members among the audience, starting with King James and Prince Charles. Then some of the gipsies (not Buckingham, though) picked the pockets of country gulls, characters who had entered the scene in the meantime. The masque culminated in the metamorphosis of the 'gipsies' into proper courtiers and concluded with more dances and a blessing of the king's five senses. Notwithstanding its high-profile audience, *The Gypsies Metamorphos'd* was a *risqué* piece which experimented with innovative features, some of them outrageous. In particular, Jonson and his artistic collaborators drew upon French-style ballet and banqueting fashions which they combined with traditional English music and song. In this essay I shall try to show why they did so.

The Gypsies Metamorphos'd departed from the customary tropes of praise lavished on king and court with a number of contentious elements. Court masques visualised the immaterial qualities of the court when noble performers impersonated allegorical deities and mythical rulers in mute dancing roles.[3] While such strategies sought to establish a distance from professional acting, Jonson's masque assigned low-class speaking roles to aristocrats. Furthermore, no music from the heavenly spheres, but a scatological ballad announced their appearance. Another offence consisted in the fact that Buckingham's gipsies had greased their faces so as to appear tawny. Masquers, however, usually wore masks of scented leather to disguise themselves, and contrary practice solicited problematic audience feedback.[4]

Ample opportunities for embarrassment lay in the fortune-telling scene. 'With you, lucky bird, I begin,' Buckingham addressed his king, reaching out for the royal hand.[5] James was allegedly not squeamish ('His skin was as soft as Taffeta Sarsnet, which felt so, because hee never washt his hands, only rub'd his fingers ends sleightly with the wet end of a Naptkin [sic],' one detractor wrote).[6] Still, Buckingham risked leaving some marks on his guest when he 'read' and kissed the royal palm, intimately alluding to the king's passion for hunting and dislike of pork meat:

> Here's a Gentlemans hand.
> I'le kisse it for luck's sake, you should by this line
> Love a horse and a hound, but no part of a swine [...].[7]

Given such details, ungenerous observers could have interpreted The Gypsies Metamorphos'd as an extended insult to the crown. As is well known, public opinion considered Buckingham a rapacious, corrupt favourite who abused his sovereign's generosity. Not only did his grace have the audacity to present himself as a leader of thieves, he even implicated the king in his plot: by audience participation, the masque gave James an air of complicity when Buckingham contaminated, perhaps even stained, the royal hand during the moment of palmreading. Jonson's masque has, for this reason, solicited uneasy critical responses, leading to the somewhat helpless conclusion that, away from Whitehall, James's court could afford to relax a little and enjoy a rude joke.[8] Yet The Gypsies Metamorphos'd was precisely tuned to occasion and audience. The masque succeeded, Martin Butler has argued, because it managed to balance Buckingham's public persona between 'ugly greedy' and 'sexy greedy'.[9] To that end, Jonson and his collaborators developed several devices which mitigated the deceptive rusticity of the event and imperceptibly gentrified it.

One strategy consisted in investing the performers with a noble genealogy in word and image. For James's court witnessed 'gentleman-like Gipsies', even 'Princes of Ægipt'. With frequent references to 'Cleopatra' Jonson's lines recall, of course, a favourite of the English stage.[10] The tanned complexion of

Shakespeare's queen betrayed her alarming 'gipsy's lust' yet made her irresistible.[11] In the same way, Jonson's masque represented Buckingham's tawny gipsies as dangerously seductive. Even palmistry has a pedigree here, when the text dates the gipsies' skills back to the Arabic scientist Al-Kindi.[12] The musical sounds evoked the countryside but also more remote, exotic locations. Throughout the performance, the audience heard the gipsies' tinkling noises. The wearing of bells is still common practice in English morris-dancing but may, in the context of this masque, allude to the more remote tradition of the *moresca* dancer. Bells (sometimes made of silver, which produces a particularly piercing sound) were used by itinerant professionals who had entered Europe via Spain by the fifteenth century (see Figure 1).[13] These dancers imported a moorish dance style which included mock battles and grotesque repertoire. Interestingly, Buckingham's gipsies had brought a guitar, then rarely used in England, which evoked a mediterranean atmosphere.[14] What exactly Buckingham would have known about the *moresca* we do not know; however, as John Forrest has shown, the term 'moresca', denoting dancing of Spanish or Moorish origins, accompanied by bells, frequently occurred in mid-seventeenth-century English dictionaries and commentaries, and indeed performers with black faces or vizards called 'Moreskoes' and 'Egipcians' have a long theatrical history in England as they can be traced back to entertainments under Henry VIII.[15]

Significantly, the country yokels in Buckingham's masque were at a loss how to define the performance of 'Ptolomee's boyes'. These should be morris-dancers, they wonder, but miss the napkins, the hobby horse, the fool and Maid Marian: 'didst thou ever see such? the finest olive-coloured sprites, they have so dancd and gingled here, as if they had beene a sett of overgrowne ffayeries'.[16] A dancing competition between the gipsies and the clowns and their girls ('if wee can, lett's dance them downe'[17]) ensues. Buckingham's crew clearly renounced a local style of morris-dancing in favour of something more unusual and remote. The (unknown) choreographer of *The Gypsies Metamorphos'd* might have looked at historicising, exotic or grotesque movements which emphasised the gipsies' oriental origins and distinguished them from rural clodhopping. The country crowd's choice of the lowly bagpipe and tabor and pipe for their own dances[18] emphasised this distinction.

It is important to consider Jonson's masque in the context of French entertainment, of which Buckingham was an ambassador.[19] In her pioneering study of French *ballet de cour*, Margaret McGowan has defined burlesque ballet as a form popular in the 1620s and early 1630s: it granted greater artistic licence to aristocratic performers; it drew upon everyday topics for social satire; it emphasised the individual's appearance and professional skills rather than sumptuous backdrops; and it was highly mobile, capable of migrating to various performance locations.[20] An early English correlative of French burlesque ballet, the *Running Masque*, a series of improvised performances, moved from one aristocratic country residence to the next during the Christmas season of 1619/20. These events involved Buckingham, Scottish courtiers and members of the King's bedchamber. The roaring boys, as they were dubbed,[21] apparently

Fig. 1. Black moresca dancer wearing bells. Wooden sculpture by Erasmus Grasser, German, late fifteenth century. Munich. Münchner Stadtmuseum, inv. no. 1c/222. © Münchner Stadtmuseum.

endorsed a French innovation, for the inveterate court gossip John Chamberlain grumbled in a letter in 1620:

[this] manner of running maske they pretend to borough from the French, (though for my part I remember no such thing in my time) but noe doubt but in all other fantasticall fashions so in this we strive to exceede and unstrip them.[22]

The *Running Masque* involved the characters of Mercury and some pickpockets. It not only predated – and probably influenced – *The Gypsies Metamorphos'd* but had an impact on a number of informal court entertainments of the early 1620s.[23] French *ballet de cour* did not insist on the rigid distinction of performers by rank in the way Jacobean court masques did. If Buckingham played a gipsy thief, he needed to move away from Whitehall, whereas high-ranking French nobility took on comparable roles in the epicentre of power at Paris. Louis XIII danced as a pickpocket in *Le Ballet du roy representant les bacchanales* (1623). A veritable ballet of thieves was performed at the Louvre in February 1624. Here the king participated as a Dutch captain, and his brother played a pirate. The Maréchal de Bassompierre, who had been Buckingham's guest in the previous year, dressed up as a 'corsair' and even recited a few lines. Various counts danced as thieves, while the Comte de Chalez impersonated a fortune teller.[24] A performance of gipsies in rural Rutlandshire seems less scandalous if it simply reflects an increasing influence of French *ballet de cour* on the English court.

It is quite possible that a French choreographer and stage designer had a hand in the organisation of the *Gypsies Metamorphos'd*. One Barthélemy de Montagut had entered Buckingham's household in 1619 or 1620. This professional not only orchestrated several entertainments for Buckingham, in which he also participated as a dancer, he also composed (under dubious circumstances) a choreographic treatise which he dedicated to his patron.[25] In 1626 Montagut danced in a French entertainment for the king and queen and the French ambassador Bassompierre, who enthused about the superb feast.[26] Buckingham, the royals, and Bassompierre himself all sat at the same table while dances, representations and changes of scenery accompanied every course. Buckingham served the King in person. The company continued with country dances until four o'clock in the morning.[27] Montagut seems to have been a specialist for choreographing so-called *charactères de la danse*, or *ballets des nations*, a topic frequent in French *ballet de cour*. He would have been Buckingham's most obvious choice for choreographing the ancient gipsy nation.

In order to evaluate Buckingham's strategy in commissioning Jonson, we need to see it in terms of Buckingham's personal tastes in festive culture, and furthermore we need to consider Buckingham's rivalry with James Hay, first Earl of Carlisle (c.1580–1636), a prominent and important figure at the Jacobean court. Buckingham's feasts were dramatic representations in their own right. Here he competed with Hay, equally notorious for ostentatious shows.[28] Both had enjoyed France in their youth and acted as powerful cultural brokers with particular interests in French ballet and banqueting practice. As Timothy Raylor explains, a seventeenth-century English 'banquet' denoted 'a light course of costly and elaborately decorated sweetmeats'.[29] Hay expanded the British culinary horizon by introducing jollifications *à la française*, detested by Chamberlain ('we are too apish to imitate the French monkeys in such monstrous waste').[30] Among the notorious inventions attributed to Hay was the antesupper (some kind of supper laid out for visual display and thrown out before the supper proper was served).[31] Hay's *Essex House Masque* in 1621, to which he had invited the French ambassador, became a byword for conspicuous display. In the course of a week, forty cooks produced 1600 different dishes including two swans. After this supper followed a banquet, then the masque, then a second banquet. This cost Hay more than £ 3000. A Jacobean craftsman would have worked for some 170 years to earn such a sum.[32] 'For Lord Hay, the food placed on the table is largely there to be wasted, and this waste confirms both his own status and that of his guests', Bruce Boehrer writes about the *Essex House Masque*: gluttony meant power in a time when ordinary households spent between four-fifths and all of their resources on food.[33]

Critics have observed the ongoing rivalry between Buckingham and Hay in the early 1620s.[34] Hay, an experienced arbiter of French taste and established court bonvivant, watched the inexorable rise of the new favourite with a wary eye. Buckingham, on the other hand, still needed to prove himself. In 1621, Buckingham could have chosen to outdo Hay's *Essex House Masque* by an even more gorgeous feast but instead commissioned Jonson to pursue a completely different strategy. Performed half a year after its rival, *The Gypsies Metamorphos'd* contrasts sharply with Hay's masque.

THE SONG OF COCK LOREL

Jonson's masque for Buckingham needs to be understood in the context of the well-known importance of 'transformation' in Jacobean entertainments, where, onstage, trees turned into dancers or statues into ladies. Hay's *Essex House Masque* provided another superlative in this respect: thanks to complicated machinery, giants were first changed into stone and then into men in a double metamorphosis.[35] *The Gypsies Metamorphos'd*, too, hinged on the transformation of gipsies into proper courtiers. Jonson's masque, however, withheld the excitement of special effects. In this most crucial scene of the masque, nothing happened at all. The main protagonists simply cleared the stage and left the audience to their own purposes. Instead of a spectacular change of costumes and setting, a simple song signposted the transformation of the (absent) gipsies into proper courtiers. To fill this moment, Jonson devised a long burlesque ballad which resounded 'like a chime' in the ears of listeners, as if to replicate the gipsies' bells, but which also recalled the particular setting of the entertainment.[36] '*Cock-Lorell* would needs have the *Divell* his guest' eventually became Jonson's most popular poem.[37] It shares the theme of banqueting with Hay's entertainment practices. The ballad describes how the legendary gipsy leader 'Cock Laurel' (originally a sixteenth-century term for 'arch-rogue') invites Satan to a cannibalistic dinner (indeed many copies of Jonson's poem bear the title *Cook Laurel* due to its culinary theme).[38] Some sixteen stanzas explain how, in the course of the banquet, the devil gobbles up a Puritan, lawyer, bawd, taylor, usurer, sheriff and many others:

> A *London* Cuckold, hot from the spitt,
> And when the Carver up had broake him,
> The Devill chopt up his head at a bit,
> But the hornes were very neare like to choake him.[39]

The music for *Cock Lorel* is unknown. As a ballad, the piece was probably sung to a popular tune. *Packington's Pound* has been suggested but a more likely score was first published in John Playford's *The English Dancing Master* (1651) under the unpromising title *An Old Man is a Bed Full of Bones*. It was first associated with Jonson's text in the 1700 edition of *Wit and Mirth*.[40] Sung to a traditional tune (whatever this may eventually have been), the ballad celebrates the eating – and purging – of a Jacobean body politic; contentious elements are digested into fumes.[41] For after the devil has washed down his meal with Derby ale, he vents a gargantuan fart, from whence, as we are told, the place is called 'The Devil's Arse'. Countryside entertainments usually played on local features of the place in which they were performed. Famously, Milton's *Comus* alludes to the river Severn, running close to Ludlow Castle where the Egerton children acted as masquers. Jonson's ballad, too, referred to a distinct landmark, the Devil's Arse Cavern below Peveril Castle, Castleton, in the Peak District of Derbyshire:

There standeth upon the top of a hill an old castle under which is a cave or hole within the ground called [...] The Devil's Arse, that gapeth with a wide mouth and hath in it many turnings and relying rooms. Notwithstanding, by reason of these and such like fables, this hole is reckoned for one of the wonders of England.[42]

Today the 'largest natural cave entrance in the British Isles' opens to a commercial attraction developed by Peak Cavern Ltd. Guided tours lead to 'Pluto's dining room' and the 'Devil's cellar', where special events still include banquets. Apparently the name 'Devil's Arse' derives from the flatulent noise the water makes when it drains away. Visitor numbers have dramatically increased since the organisers changed the prim Victorian misnomer of the site ('Peak Cavern') back to the original in 2001.[43] Jonson, too, clearly felt inspired by the cave's name (he mentioned it more than once in his works).[44] Cock Lorel's subterranean palace forms the centre of the masque although, geographically speaking, the Devil's Arse is more than forty miles away from Burley (and Belvoir) where *The Gypsies Metamorphos'd* was performed. Jonson's text gentrifies the traditional location by having the arch-rogue hold court in a 'Pallace of the Peake', more in line with Buckingham's illustrious audience.

With his ballad, Jonson also addressed a personal concern in *The Gypsies Metamorphos'd*. His work, Bruce Boehrer argues,

absorbs a popular Jacobean strategy for social aggrandisement: conspicuous con-sumption in the name of an all-powerful and all-virtuous monarch. [...] The dishes reserved for great men's feasts become Jonson's own conceptual and linguistic property.[45]

In many of Jonson's masques, food turned into actors for a celebration of all five senses. *The Christmas Masque* (1616) presented a minced pie, dressed 'like a fine cook's wife', and a baby cake 'like a boy, in a fine long coat, biggin, bib, muckender, and a little dagger'.[46] For *Neptune's Triumph* (1624), Jonson invented a dance of ingredients coming out of a pot and a Cook who laid out the recipe for a good masque:

> there is a palate of the understanding, as well as of the senses. The taste is taken with good relishes, the sight with fair objects, the hearing with delicate sounds, the smelling with pure scents, the feeling with soft and plump bodies, but the understanding with all these; for all which you must begin at the kitchen. There the art of poetry was learned [...] the same day with the art of cookery.[47]

Cock Lorel's Rabelaisian banquet provided an anarchic foil to Jonson's culinary court masques as here the characters turned into food, not vice versa. *Neptune's Triumph* had denigrated ballads as 'abortive and extemporal din' which disturbed the proper *déroulement* of a court masque.[48] In a radical inversion, *The Gypsies Metamorphos'd* relied on popular song as a key element to understanding the performance. *Cock Lorel* debunked encomiastic excess and spectacle as merely flatulent. The devil's dinner sniped at French feasts, and the timing of the ballad – at the point of the gipsies' apotheosis – unmasked stage pyrotechnics as unnecessary, tortuous ploys. For once and all, the masque established that it was not choice foods but the presence of the king which made the entertainment great, in line with Jonson's poem 'Inviting a Friend to Supper':

> It is the faire acceptance, Sir, creates
> The entertaynment perfect: not the cates.[49]

Such ideas of civilised entertainment also recall Jonson's *leges conviviales* which applied to the regular gatherings of his circle in London's Apollo Tavern, including 'Let the dishes be prepared rather with respect to their distinction than to expense'.[50] In this way, *The Gypsies Metamorphos'd* articulated Jonsonian ideas of moderation as they applied to both dining and masque-making.

A simple tune, then, entertained the audience on a nearly empty stage.[51] While long stanzas expatiated on the devil's menu, the gipsies hastily rubbed off their make-up and put on rich garments. Having been a well-tanned vagabond a few minutes ago, Buckingham re-emerged all pale perfection. The text makes clear that the reformed gipsy's is the real persona, since only after his transformation Buckingham's actual name is mentioned for the first time.[52] After the ballad which had ended in a foul-smelling fart, the gipsies' panegyric sets a textual, visual and olfactory counterpoint:

> Looke, looke, is he not faire,
> And fresh, and fragrant too.
> As summers skie or pured aire,
> And lookes as lillies doe [...].[53]

'You have beheld (and with delight) theire change,' Jonson's epilogue tells the audience. It refers to the result rather than process, since the transformation was exactly what the audience did not see. Buckingham's and Jonson's countryside vision provocatively commented on grand court masques which hinged on eye-popping visual effects for the onstage apotheosis of aristocratic dancers. *The Gypsies Metamorphos'd* appealed much more economically to the audience's five senses when words and music evoked colours and smells (a strategy re-affirmed at the end when King James's five senses were praised). In Jonson's plain masque the hippopotamus was for once not rolling the pea. ''Twas truth [...] And no device':[54] instead of cranking up the machinery, Jonson simply asked his guests to use their imagination. The metamorphosis into an ideal courtier came so naturally to Buckingham, the text suggested, that an explanation was irrelevant: it was 'not touchd at by our Poet; Good *Ben* slept there, or else forgot to showe it'.[55]

By the end of the masque, the text had established that Buckingham's fortunes were entirely dependent on the king's grace. Like his rival Hay, who returned his bounty 'whence it came from'[56], Buckingham prettily attributed his luck to James's generosity:

> My selfe a *Gypsye* here doe shine,
> Yet are you Maker, Sir, of mine.
> Ô that Confession would content
> So highe a bountie, that doth knowe
> No part of motion but to flowe,
> And givinge never to repent.[57]

Buckingham's crew playfully restored their spoils to the victims. The thief, it seems, was in the eye of the beholder, and Jonson's masque corrected the audience's perception in all five senses. Making a show of his intimacy with the king, Buckingham proved that, dressed as the meanest vagrant, he may still touch and kiss the royal hand. As Butler concludes, Jonson's masque playfully questioned the favourite's integrity, but under the benevolent eye of the king, the favourite was found to be above suspicion. Relaxed as the event seemed, Buckingham had passed a survival test.[58]

Half a year after Hay's excesses, *The Gypsies Metamorphos'd* presented a jocular scene of culinary overkill. The creative energy of Jonson's food imagery demonstrated that Buckingham did not need 1600 dishes to impress the court and kiss the king's hand. Not even an apotheosis was required to prove Buckingham's position. In *The Gypsies Metamorphos'd* French traditions of dancing and dining, English folklore, and Jonsonian ideals of masquing were not mutually exclusive but provided a compelling menu of contrasts which maximised the protagonists' expressive range. The masque brilliantly illustrated the anarchic fluidity between Continental and local culture and thus reconciled seemingly incompatible positions: that of semi-professional exotic dancer and English aristocrat, thief and favourite, king and gipsy.

ACKNOWLEDGEMENTS

I am most grateful to Richard Sugg for his helpful comments on this essay, and would like to thank Dr Michael Teichmann, Münchner Stadtmuseum, for his support.

NOTES

1. *The Gypsies Metamorphos'd* was performed three times in 1621: at Burley-on-the-Hill on 3 August; at Belvoir, Leicestershire, on 5 August; and at Windsor, probably in early September, in a revised version. *Ben Jonson [Works]*, ed. by C. H. Herford, Percy and Evelyn Simpson, 11 vols (Oxford: Clarendon Press, 1925–52), X, p. 541. Hereafter abbreviated as H&S.
2. H&S VII, p. 594, l. 865.
3. See Stephen Orgel's classic study *The Jonsonian Masque* (New York: Columbia University Press, 1981; repr. of 1967 edn with new introduction).
4. B. Ravelhofer, *The Early Stuart Masque: Dance, Costume, and Music* (Oxford: Oxford University Press, 2006), ch. 7.
5. H&S VII, p. 574, l. 275.
6. A. Weldon, *The Court and Character of King James* (London: R. I. and John Wright, 1650), p. 178; an account to be taken with a pinch of salt. H&S X, p. 621.
7. H&S VII, p. 574, ll. 278–80.
8. For example, Dale B. Randall's classic study, *Jonson's Gypsies Unmasked: Background and Theme of 'The Gypsies Metamorphos'd'* (Durham, North Carolina: Duke University Press, 1975), registers unease with Jonson's masque.
9. Martin Butler, '"We are one mans all": Jonson's *The Gipsies Metamorphosed*', *Yearbook of English Studies*, 21 (1991), 253–73, p. 258.
10. H&S VII, p. 567, ll. 58–62; p. 590, l. 753.
11. Stephen Orgel, 'Marginal Jonson', in *The Politics of the Stuart Court Masque*, David Bevington and Peter Holbrook (eds) (Cambridge: Cambridge University Press, 1998), pp. 144–75, at 161. Philo on Cleopatra's 'gipsy's lust' in *Antony and Cleopatra*, I.1.10.
12. H&S VII, p. 571, l. 184.
13. For a concise history see Johanna Müller-Meiningen, *Die Moriskentänzer und andere Arbeiten des Erasmus Grasser für das Alte Rathaus in München* (Regensburg: Schnell und Steiner, 1998).
14. Bills also mention fiddlers and a cornet-player (H&S X, p. 613); yet their purpose is unclear. As Peter Walls points out, the *OED* lists Jonson's masque as the first reference to 'guitar' in English; the instrument must have been thought suitably exotic for the gipsies. *Music in the English Courtly Masque, 1604–1640* (Oxford: Clarendon Press, 1996), p. 274. The guitar became established in medieval Spain; Spanish and Italian composers first popularised the instrument across Europe. James Tyler, 'The Guitar and Its Performance from the Fifteenth to Eighteenth Centuries', *Performance Practice Review*, X/1 (1997), 61–70.
15 John Forrest, *The History of Morris Dancing, 1458–1750* (Cambridge: Clarke, 1999), pp. 6, 367 (with reference to a royal Shrovetide banquet in 1510).
16 H&S VII, p. 589, ll. 732–7.
17 H&S VII, p. 591, ll. 796–7.
18 H&S VII, p. 590, ll. 772–3. Walls, p. 150.
19 For a general comparative analysis see Marie-Claude Canova-Green, *La politique-spectacle au grand siècle: les rapports franco-anglais*, biblio 17 (Paris: Papers on French Seventeenth-Century Literature, 1993).
20 Margaret M. McGowan's pioneering study, *L'art du ballet de cour en France, 1581–1643* (Paris: Éditions du centre national de la recherche scientifique, 1963), ch. 8, and *The Court Ballet of Louis XIII* (London: Victoria and Albert Museum, [1994]). Mark Franko, *Dance as Text: Ideologies of the Baroque Body* (Cambridge: Cambridge University Press, 1993), ch. 4.
21 H&S VII, p. 585, l. 627.

22. To Dudley Carleton, 8 January 1620, cited from James Knowles, 'The *Running Masque Recovered*: A Masque for the Marquess of Buckingham (c.1619–20)', *English Manuscript Studies*, 8 (2000), 79–135, p. 119.

23. Knowles, p. 85.

24. R. Bordier, *Vers pour le ballet des voleurs* (Paris: Jean Serra, 1624).

25. B. de Montagut, *Louange de la danse*, B. Ravelhofer (ed.) (Cambridge: RTM, 2000), introduction.

26. *Louange de la danse*, p. 14.

27. François de Bassompierre, *Journal de ma vie*, M. de Chantérac (ed.), vol. III (Paris, 1875), p. 274.

28. Hay, a Scottish courtier, was created Earl of Carlisle in September 1622.

29. Timothy Raylor (ed.), *The Essex House Masque of 1621: Viscount Doncaster and the Jacobean Masque* (Pittsburgh: Duquesne University Press, 2000), p. 53.

30. *Louange*, p. 10. To Carleton, London, 22 February 1617.

31. I am grateful to Anne Barton for discussing Hay's culinary exploits.

32. Raylor, p. 76, citing Chamberlain to Carleton, 13 January 1621; statistics after E. II. Brown Phelps and Sheila V. Hopkins, 'Seven Centuries of Building Wages', in *Essays in Economic History*, ed. by E. M. Carus-Wilson, 3 vols (London: 1954–62), II, pp. 168–78.

33. Bruce Thomas Boehrer, *The Fury of Men's Gullets: Ben Jonson and the Digestive Canal* (Philadelphia: University of Pennsylvania Press, 1997), pp. 84–5, 98.

34. Raylor, pp. 112–13, 118.

35. Raylor's *Essex House Masque*, introduction, part 1 and 2.

36. H&S VII, p. 600, l. 1049.

37. H&S VII, p. 601, l. 1062; X, p. 633. Peter Beal, *Index of English Literary Manuscripts*, 2 vols (London: Mansell, 1980–93).

38. H&S X, p. 629.

39. H&S VII, p. 602, ll. 1098–1101. In subsequent performances Jonson added stanzas.

40. *Packington's Pound* (H&S X, p. 635) is too long to accommodate the four-line stanzas of Jonson's text. Since it offers the earliest combination of music and text, Andrew Sabol privileges 'A Ballad call'd Cook-Lorrel, The Words by Ben Jonson', in *Wit and Mirth or, Pills to purge Melancholy*, collected by Henry Playford and Thomas D'Urfey, 2 vols (London: W. Pearson for H. Playford, 1699, 1700), p. 101. This treble tune goes well with the text and represents a version of 'An Old Man Is a Bed Full of Bones' in *The English Dancing Master* (1651). *The English Dancing Master (1651)*, Hugh Mellor and Leslie Bridgewater (eds) (London: Dance Books, 1984), p. 76, and *Four Hundred Songs and Dances from the Stuart Masque*, Andrew J. Sabol (ed.) (Hanover, London: University Press of New England, 1982), pp. 103, 556–7. I am grateful to Henk Dragstra for discussing the musical sources for Jonson's ballad.

41. 'Eating people is not wrong at the Devil's Arse cavern,' Butler remarks, 'since the figures on whom the devil dines are all middle-class types the symbolic digesting of whom is likelier to have amused the king than angered him' (p. 262).

42. William Camden, *Britannia* (London: Newbery, 1586; repr. Hildesheim, New York: Olms, 1974).

43. Visitor numbers have risen by more than 30% since the name change: ananova.com/news/story/sm_383491.html?menu=news.quirkies; BBC news, Friday, 6 July 2001, at news.bbc.co.uk/hi/english/uk/newsid_1425000/1425909.stm. For images of the cave, see www.peakcavern.co.uk.

44. For instance, in *The Devil Is an Ass* (1616) and *The Entertainment at Welbeck* (1633). I am grateful to Eugene Giddens for these references, as for other most helpful comments on this essay.

45. Boehrer, pp. 96–7.

46. *Court Masques*, David Lindley (ed.) (Oxford: Oxford University Press, 1995), p. 110, ll. 5–6, 52–4.

47. *Neptune's Triumph, Court Masques*, p. 137, ll. 41–7.

48. *Neptune's Triumph, Court Masques*, p. 139, l. 117.

49. Folio edition (1640), ll. 7–8. 'Cates' are choice foods. I am grateful to Anne Barton for this

reference.

50. Boehrer's translation from the Latin text (pp. 68–9).
51. Butler, p. 255. To the ballad, 149 lines of dialogue between the 'patrico' (some kind of hedge-priest) and country people must be added.
52. H&S VII, p. 608, l. 1278.
53. H&S VII, p. 613, ll. 1418–21.
54. H&S VII, p. 608, ll. 1293–4.
55. H&S VII, p. 615, ll. 1475–8. 'Not only does the metamorphosis fail to grow naturally and inevitably out of the action of the masque, but Jonson is at pains to point up its arbitrariness and inexplicability,' Raylor writes about this passage (p. 118). Raylor's work is brilliantly sensitive to the lack of motivation in the transformation scene, but I think Jonson did not wish to highlight a weakness in the plot – rather he points out that Buckingham's fabulous metamorphosis requires no artifice and no motivation. Furthermore, the phrase 'Good *Ben* slept there' is an allusion to the Horatian 'bonus dormitat Homerus' (H&S X, p. 633). Jonson confidently associates himself with classical authorities here; nothing could be further removed from an excuse.
56. Hay's motto was 'redit unde fuit'.
57. H&S VII, p. 576, ll. 340–5.
58. Butler also notices that the gipsies restore their spoils (p. 257).

From Tragicomedy to Epic: The Court Ballets of Desmarets de Saint-Sorlin

MARIE-CLAUDE CANOVA-GREEN

It was customary in the seventeenth century to assimilate court ballet with drama, as both art forms were seen to strive for a common aim: the imitation or representation of nature. However, critics were also keen to point out their essential differences, for, unlike tragedy, ballet disregarded the rules of neo-classical aesthetics and its only concern seemed to be to please and to entertain. This was particularly evident in the court ballets written by Desmarets de Saint-Sorlin between 1639 and 1641. Unsurprisingly, they were singled out for special criticism by theorists of the ballet, who highlighted their dramatic shortcomings, and failed to see that they constituted another form of dramatic aesthetics, which was conspicuous precisely because of its emancipation from the strictures of Aristotelian theory. It could be said that the ballets of Desmarets had all the hallmarks of contemporary tragicomedy: irregularity of construction, diversity of action, disregard for the unity of tone, etc., but in adapting the principles of this new aesthetics to the ballet, Desmarets ran the risk of transgressing the boundaries of tragicomedy and even of drama, approaching a genre which was no longer dramatic but narrative, i.e. epic poetry.

As Margaret M. McGowan has shown,[1] court ballet originated in France at the end of the sixteenth century as a conscious union of four different art forms: dance, music, poetry, and painting. From its inception it was analysed within the framework of an aesthetics based on a system of correspondences between the arts. On the one hand poetry and painting, already associated by Horace in his *Ars poetica*,[2] now jointly defined the art of dancing, seen as a 'peinture agissante'[3] or a 'poësie animée'.[4] According to Guillaume Colletet,

Si les anciens ont appelé la Poësie une peinture parlante, et la Peinture une poësie muette, à leur exemple nous pouvons appeler la Dance, et surtout celle qui se pratique dans nos Ballets, une peinture mouvante, ou une poësie animée. Car comme la Poësie est un vray tableau de nos passions, et la Peinture un discours muet veritablement, mais capable neantmoins de reveiller tout ce qui tombe dans nostre imagination: ainsi la Dance est une image vivante de nos actions, et une expression artificielle de nos secrettes pensées.[5]

On the other hand, ballet, 'l'espece la plus parfaite' of dance,[6] was soon assimilated to drama. For the Abbé de Pure, it was a 'Fable müette',[7] a silent representation, 'où les gestes & les mouvemens signifient ce qu'on pourroit exprimer par des paroles'.[8] The Jesuit Ménestrier even remarked:

Et pour me servir des rapports de la poësie pour les distinguer je compare la simple dance aux vers lyriques qui n'ont rien d'arresté pour le dessein & le Ballet au poëme dramatique qui a un Intrigue & diverses operations qui sont developpées par un dénoüement, & conduites par les incidens des passions.[9]

The underlying reason being that, transcending the medium used, all forms of art strive for a common aim, which was the imitation or representation of nature.

But this traditional comparison between ballet and drama was problematic. Ménestrier himself only used it to underline their essential differences.[10] In his opinion nothing but their common mimetic aim could ever justify their being likened. Unlike tragedy, with which it was nearly always compared, ballet did not comply with the rules of French neo-classical drama, as established during the seventeenth century. It disregarded the sacrosanct principles of *vraisemblance* (verisimilitude), *bienséances* (decorum) and the unities,[11] and instead followed the law of 'l'agréable' and 'l'ingénieux'. Indeed what could be further removed from neo-classical aesthetics than a composition of which it was said that 'n'ayant jamais esté reglé par les Anciens, on en a fait une piece de Caprice ou l'on se donne beaucoup de liberté'?[12]

However, what Ménestrier and others failed to consider was that some of the characteristics of ballet did constitute a form of dramatic aesthetics, albeit different from the theory and practice of mid seventeenth-century France. This was particularly evident in the two ballets written by Desmarets de Saint-Sorlin in 1639–1641, which Ménestrier singled out for special criticism in his *Remarques pour la conduite des ballets*. This form of dramatic aesthetics was conspicuous precisely for its emancipation from the strictures of Aristotelian theory and for its demands for literary freedom. In other words the main features of the ballets of Desmarets could be related to those of tragicomic drama. For tragicomedy was not just about the combination of the comic and the tragic on stage, the disregard of the unity of tone. It was characterised above all by the irregularity of its construction, the diversity of the events represented, and the hedonistic nature of its aim.

This was the aesthetics that Desmarets de Saint-Sorlin helped formulate in the mid to late 1630s[13] and adopted in four of his plays: *Scipion* (1638), *Roxane* (1639), *Erigone* (1639), and *Mirame* (1641). This was also the aesthetics he claimed to follow in the preface to the *Ballet de la Félicité* (1639), and on which both this ballet and the later *Ballet de la Prospérité des Armes de France* (1641) were in part modelled. Although *Europe*, his third contribution to the pleasures of the court of Louis XIII, was not a ballet but an allegorical piece, entitled 'comédie héroïque', it also fulfilled some of the same criteria. But, in multiplying to excess the variety and the diversity of the actions represented on stage, in overstretching the theoretical coincidence between actual time and fictional time, Desmarets ran the risk of transgressing the boundaries of tragicomedy and even of drama, and approached a genre which was no longer dramatic but narrative, i.e. epic poetry.

As a dramatist, Desmarets could not but subscribe to the comparison between ballet and drama. In his opening remarks to the *Ballet de la Prospérité des Armes de France* in 1641 he stated that:

Les Ballets sont des comedies muettes, et doivent estre divisés de mesme par actes et par scenes. Les recits separent les actes, et les entrées de danseurs sont autant de scenes.[14]

It was first of all by its *dispositio* that the ballet resembled a play, since it was similarly divided into acts and scenes. The number of acts (or parts, as they were generally called) in Desmarets's ballets was consonant with tradition for tragedy and tragicomedy: whereas the *Ballet de la Félicité* was divided into three parts,[15] in a clear attempt to reproduce the conventional tripartite division of the dramatic action into beginning, middle and end,[16] the *Ballet de la Prospérité des Armes de France* was divided into five acts, and was thus much more in line with the formal requirements of the neo-classical play.[17] Hence the critical remarks of Marolles and Ménestrier regarding the unusual composition of the latter ballet:

Les parties font la division du Ballet, elles sont arbitraires pour le nombre, neantmoins on ne va gueres jusqu'à cinq, comme la Tragedie.[18]

As both critics noted, a three-part division was considered to be the norm for major court ballets:

Il faut que la division se reduise en moins de Parties que faire se peut. Les Maistres n'en permettent au plus que trois.[19]

As for the number of scenes (or entries) per act, it varied between eight and ten for the *Ballet de la Félicité*, and six and nine for the *Ballet de la Prospérité*,[20] in accordance again with contemporary dramatic practice.

Unlike his predecessors at court, Desmarets also endeavoured to ensure the *liaison* of scenes, recommended by all theorists of the theatre for the good order and arrangement of the dramatic material, but deemed unnecessary or even inoperative in the case of ballet, which only required 'unité de dessein'.[21] The Abbé Michel de Pure thought it necessary to remind his readers of

une différence des Entrées de Balet, & des Scenes du Poëme dramatique. Car en celuy-cy les Scenes doivent estre liées entr'elles, au lieu qu'en celuy-là il suffit qu'elles le soient au sujet. Celle qui finit n'a que faire avec celle qui doit commencer apres elle.[22]

Still this liaison was desirable if it could be achieved without detracting from the necessary 'judicieuse diversité' of the entries.[23] De Pure added:

Il est toutefois avantageux pour Elles [i.e. les entrées], & pour le Sujet, qu'elles soient bien liées entr'elles: & que la suite fasse une espece d'anchaînement, comme indivisible. Cette liaison se fait avec plus de facilité & plus de perfection par le moyen des Incidents, & lors que l'Entrée est un progrez ou un embarras de celle qui a precedé, ou une preparation pour celle qui suit.[24]

In his two court ballets, Desmarets constructed genuine sequences of three, four, or even more entries, which developed a continuous action, an incident which formed part of the main action, and did not even clear the stage between them. For example, the sequences showing the wars between European nations and the hostile endeavours of the Turks in the *Ballet de la Félicité*, or those featuring the sieges of Casale and Arras in the *Ballet de la Prospérité des Armes de France*. Admittedly not all entries were linked together, nor were they all related to the central theme. Indeed Ménestrier claimed not to be able to find the subject of the *Ballet de la Prospérité des Armes de France* in the entries of Tritons, Nereids, Muses, Apollo, Mercury, Jupiter, Cardelin, Spanish men and women dancing, or Americans bringing their treasures to Spain, and even questioned the liaison of acts and scenes in the ballet.[25]

But if the entries had become dramatic sequences, even genuine scenes imitative of an action, it was logical that the few songs and dances inserted in the ballets should be placed in the position of interludes, i.e. in the intervals, on the external margins of the works, precisely where the dramatic theorists thought they ought to be. In this way their function as entertainments was highlighted. In its antepenultimate entry, the second part of the *Ballet de la Félicité* included a 'chanson à boire', followed by a masquerade, while the third part of the same ballet concluded with dances of Biscayens and Biscayennes to the tune of a 'chanson à danser', which replaced the traditional final *grand ballet*. The *grand ballet* was similarly absent from the finale of the *Ballet de la Prospérité des Armes de France*, which ended with an empty stage and the ascent of Gloire in a cloud machine.

The way in which Desmarets considered the *récits*, the spoken (or sung recitative style) pieces of verse which opened each of the different parts of the ballet, and whose role and function had always been one of explanation,[26] was also indicative of his training as a dramatist. For he chose to lay the stress on their function as a structuring device. To say, as he did in the preface to the *Ballet de la Prospérité des Armes de France*, that 'les recits separent les actes' was tantamount to saying that the *récits* were related to the chorus of ancient Greek tragedy, which also served to 'marquer les Intervalles des Actes'[27] and the pauses in the action. Indeed according to Aristotle, the act, or 'episode', was none other than 'tout ce qui est entre deux chants du Choeur'.[28] Desmarets also implicitly modified the explanatory function of the *récits* and assimilated them to the interventions of the tragic chorus rather than to the narratives of neo-classical drama, for example where his *récits* served to reveal the motives behind the action (*récit* of Ambition) or to convey the 'ressentiment [des] coeurs' of the French people (*récit* of Félicité), rather than provide a straightforward explanation of the forthcoming action.[29]

The ballets of Desmarets approximated drama, and more precisely French neo-classical tragedy, not only by their *dispositio*, but also by their *inventio*. Just as tragedy borrowed its subjects from history or mythology, and favoured the 'Actions de Rois, de grans Princes, de Princesses, & de Gouuerneurs d'Empires, qui ioüissent d'vn grand bonheur auant leur renuersement',[30] Desmarets drew his inspiration from contemporary history, and staged the latest and most remarkable incidents of the Thirty Years War. The obvious difference was in the type of historical material chosen, since current affairs now took the place of ancient or legendary situations. The *Ballet de la Prospérité des Armes de la France* made references to events that had taken place during the previous twelve months, such as the sieges of Casale and Arras, or the naval battle of Cadix, while the *Ballet de la Félicité* made use of the recent siege of Brisach.

But it was in the way history was treated that Desmarets's ballets most noticeably deviated from contemporary neo-classical tragedy. There was little attempt to simplify the historical data, and episodes were brought close together regardless of the resulting transgression of the dramatic unities. As Ménestrier remarked,

La Tragedie a une Scene fixe & arrétée dans une chambre, dans un Palais, dans un appartement, dans un jardin, & tout au plus dans une Ville: Le Ballet peut faire des changemens de Scene à toutes les parties, & méme à toutes les entrées. [...] La Tragedie ne represente qu'une seule action, le Ballet en reçoit plusieurs.[31]

Ballet and tragedy also differed with regard to the nature of the subject and the emotional response it was meant to provoke from the spectators. Aristotle had stated that the tragic plot had to involve a change from good fortune to ill fortune, if it was to arouse pity or fear in the audience.[32] In Desmarets's ballets, however, this change of fortune, or *peripety*,[33] became a change not from prosperity to misery, but from misery to prosperity. To quote Desmarets,

Ce Ballet [*de la Félicité*] est divisé en trois parties [...]. La premiere represente les malheurs passés de la guerre; la seconde, le bonheur present de cette naissance, et la troisiesme, celuy que l'on espere par une paix generale à l'imitation des belles tragi-comédies, qui de l'infortune et du milieu mesme du desespoir font naistre agreablement la joye et le repos.[34]

The change of direction was rendered necessary by the need to arouse entirely different emotions from the ones traditionally sought by tragedy. Admiration, and possibly a sense of relief, were now the emotions required for the new cathartic experience generated by the performance.

Still, the conduct of the action in the *Ballet de la Félicité* was far from regular, since the *peripety*, which normally signaled the denouement, took place as early as the end of Part I, with the appearance of the infant Dauphin, who was seen to put an immediate end to all the discords of Europe. The *Ballet de la Prospérité* followed a slightly different pattern in that it showed not so much changes of fortune as sudden changes of direction, or *péripéties*,[35] that is a rebounding of the action consequent upon some surprising incident or 'coup de théâtre'. One such *péripétie* was the unexpected return of the allegorical eagle and lions in the fifth entry of Act IV,[36] which marked the renewal of the fighting between France and her enemies. The denouement was only made possible by the introduction of a *deus ex machina*, in other words the intervention of Jupiter at the end of Act IV, who, in urging the Gallic Hercules to moderation, ensured the definitive restoration of peace and prosperity on the Continent.

But not everybody agreed on the terminology to be used to describe a dramatic work whose action was based on a happy change of fortune. For some contemporary critics, the term 'tragi-comédie' employed by Desmarets was improperly used. According to La Mesnardière, this type of 'Auanture de

Théatre, où les malheurs sont effacez par quelque bon éuénement'[37] was only a variant of classical tragedy, more accurately described as 'tragédie à fin heureuse'. D'Aubignac remarked similarly that ' celuy [i.e. le nom] de *Tragédie* ne signifie pas moins les Poëmes qui finissent par la joye, quand on y décrit les fortunes des personnes illustres',[38] and added that to call this kind of drama 'tragi-comédie' resulted in the removal of the element of surprise, because it revealed the nature of the denouement before the play had even started. In the preface to *Scipion* (1639), Desmarets himself admitted that, although the play was not in any way comic,

il valloit mieux se seruir de ce nom [i.e. tragi-comédie] apres tant d'autres, que de faire vn party à part; & suiure la mode telle qu'elle est, que d'estre seul à suiure les anciens en chose de si peu de consequence.[39]

Whether the generic term used by Desmarets to categorise the work was entirely justified or not, it was nonetheless clear that the *Ballet de la Félicité*, as well as its companion piece, the *Ballet de la Prospérité des Armes de France*, came within the irregular aesthetics of tragicomedy, as developed in France in the 1620s to 1630s in the face of opposition from the partisans of neo-classical tragedy. The complexity of the dramatic action, the variety and diversity of the events represented, with their mixture of perils and victories, concern and relief, notably in the *Ballet de la Prospérité des Armes de France*, which featured several episodes from the Thirty Years War, were all in keeping with the nature of the tragicomedies performed on the public stage in the 1630s. In a humorous listing of the main characteristics of the genre, Desmarets stressed the 'amas de grands euenemens, Capables d'employer les plus beaux ornemens',[40] just as they proved capable of holding the spectators' attention thanks to the frequent changes of direction and reversals of the action as it developed. It was hardly surprising then that, with its complex and complicated plot,

qui dans chaque Scene, monstre quelque chose de nouueau; qui tient tousiours l'esprit suspendu; & qui par cent moyens surprenans, arriue insensiblement à sa fin.[41]

tragicomedy came to be seen by a whole generation of young dramatists, as infinitely superior to regular tragedy.

The wide variety of incidents and effects in the tragicomic play was often supported by a corresponding diversity of time and place, which further infringed the rule of the unities. This in turn was accentuated by the spectacular nature of the performance, with its transformation scenes, illusionistic scenery, and complicated machinery. In this respect too, Desmarets's ballets were in keeping with the irregular aesthetics of contemporary tragicomedy. In the *Ballet de la Prospérité des Armes de France*, the vision of snow-capped mountains alternated with that of flat lands, the representation of the siege of Arras followed that of Casale, and the reenactment of the naval battle between the French and the Spanish fleets off the coast of Cadix led to the final ascent of Gloire in a cloud machine. In the *Ballet de la Félicité*, fighting European soldiers left the stage to scheming Janissaries and Bachas only to return moments later to resume their

fighting, as if to illustrate the remarks made in 1637 by the anonymous author of
the *Discours à Cliton*:

Le Theatre ne differe en rien d'une table d'attente, tout le Ciel est sa perspective, la terre
et la mer en sont les confins, et ce qu'on fait en Orient et en Occident y peut estre
representé.[42]

The action could easily be transported from Paris to Constantinople, since

tout cela peut estre imité et representé, et comme les lieux seront discernés par les diverses
faces du Theatre, les temps le pourront estre par les Scenes et par les Actes raisonnable-
ment et proportionnément, c'est à dire, eu égard à la naturelle distance des pays, et au
temps legitime qui s'est passé aux evenemens et circonstances de la vraye histoire.[43]

Besides, according to the same author,

Si vous ostez de la Scene ceste pluralité & diversité de temps, d'actions et de lieux, vous
n'y pourrez mettre les grandes histoires.[44]

Having opted for what was precisely a 'grande histoire', that is the great actions
and 'nobles desseins'[45] of the French king, Desmarets had little choice but to
adopt, at least in part, the aesthetics of tragicomedy in his ballets.

   In addition, because the stage was an image of life, it could virtually
represent anything and everything, and therefore allow the mixture of 'choses
graues auec les moins serieuses, en vne mesme suitte de discours'.[46] To object to
this mixture was to ignore 'la condition de la vie des hommes, de qui les iours &
les heures sont bien souuent entrecoupées de ris & de larmes, de contentement
& d'affliction, selon qu'ils sont agitez de la bonne ou de la mauuaise fortune'.[47]
In other words the dramatic action with a happy ending was also mixed. Matters
of state could alternate with everyday concerns, solemn dances with burlesque
antics, and noble characters with low born or amusing protagonists.[48] Standard
practice in court ballets, and even recommended by Saint-Hubert in his *Maniere
de composer et faire reussir les ballets*,[49] the alternation of the serious and the grotesque
also had its place in tragicomic drama, where it served as the expression of the
diversity of life. In the *Ballet de la Prospérité des Armes de France*, rejoicing satyrs
and acrobats could alternate with French generals because all were a sign of
the victorious endeavours (and their consequences) that the ballet celebrated.
Similarly, in the *Ballet de la Félicité*, gamblers and drinkers appeared in the wake
of soldiers to mark the return of peace and unity brought about by the birth of
the Dauphin.

   The emphasis on pleasure in the *Ballet de la Prospérité des Armes de France*, in
particular on the relaxation and recreation afforded by the performance, as a
legitimate aim of the ballet, also tied in with tragicomic aesthetics. In his preface
to Maréchal's tragicomedy *Tyr et Sidon* (1628), Ogier had justified the variety of
incidents represented by saying that only it could generate the 'plaisir' and the
'diuertissement',[50] which, in his opinion, were the true purpose of dramatic
poetry to the exclusion of the didactic and moralising function put forward by
the partisans of regular theatre. *Divertire* prevailed over *docere*. Admittedly the
feelings meant to be experienced by the spectators of court entertainments were

not just pleasure and delight, they were also admiration and even awe for the glorious deeds of the French king, whose grandeur was further enhanced by the spectacular possibilities offered by the latest developments of Baroque theatre.[51] Desmarets, the dramatist, was primarily an admiring and grateful subject of his king. What is more, he was also one of Cardinal Richelieu's protégés, and therefore a paid servant of the regime.

This might explain Desmarets's desire to take to new heights the praise of the French king, to extol his actions and his merits, in a manner never attempted before. His propagandistic programme was outlined in the dedication 'Au roi' of *Mirame*, which was performed for the grand opening of the new *salle des spectacles* at the Palais Cardinal in January 1641:

Mirame que ie presente auec respect à vostre Majesté n'a seruy que d'vn essay auant que d'y chanter ses loüanges, & si mon trauail a esté suiuy de quelque heureux succés en vn suiet inuenté, elle iugera, s'il luy plaist, de ce que ie pourray faire en parlant de ses exploits veritables. Dés-ja les Ballets que l'on y a veus depuis sa representation, n'ont eu pour sujet que les victoires de vostre Majesté, & tous leurs recits n'ont parlé que des merueilles de sa vie. Mais i'ose luy dire encore, que ie prepare vn ouurage sur le suiet de la Iustice de ses armes, & de la moderation d'vn si grand Roy, dans ses glorieux succés, qui auec l'ayde de la renommée de vostre Majesté, volera comme j'espere par tout le monde.[52]

This declaration has been seen as a blueprint for *Europe*, Desmarets's subsequent theatrical venture for the court in the autumn of 1641, which justified the diplomatic and military interventions of Louis XIII and his minister Richelieu in the Thirty Years War, from the siege of La Rochelle to the more recent successes at Perpignan, Tortone and Sedan. But in doing so, Desmarets ran the risk of overstretching the dramatic action, of overstepping the external *dispositio* and exceeding the standard duration of a theatrical performance. The *Ballet de la Félicité* was in three parts, the *Ballet de la Prospérité des Armes de la France* in five, already the maximum allowed for such works, while *Europe* included five acts and a lengthy prologue with dance (?) and music.[53] But *Europe* was not a ballet, it was an allegorical play, entitled 'comédie héroïque', a generic term later reused by Corneille for *Dom Sanche* to describe 'a Poëme dramatique [...] dont tout le Sujet fust heroïque et la fin heureuse'.[54]

    Besides, as recommended by the anonymous author of the *Discours à Cliton*, the historical subject chosen for *Europe* and the resulting amount of material used could and even ought to be the subject matter of epic poetry

tant pour le respect des personnes souveraines qui en peuvent estre, que pour éviter une longue suitte d'advantures, dont le recit ennuyeux ou la trop lente execution [peut] déplaire aux Auditeurs.[55]

This recommendation was in line with Aristotelian teaching:

It is the special advantage of epic that it may be of considerable length. [...] epic poetry, [...] being narrative, is able to represent many incidents that are being simultaneously enacted, and, provided they are relevant, they increase the weight of the poem, and give it merits of grandeur, variety of interest, and diversity in its episodes.[56]

Where ballet and tragicomedy failed, epic succeeded.

Europe was to be Desmarets's last contribution to court entertainments. Whether it was a result of the changed political situation (the successive deaths of Richelieu and Louis XIII in December 1642 and March 1643 effectively put an end to all court performances), or the realisation of the aesthetic deadlock in which he found himself, Desmarets did not compose any more ballets or allegorical plays for the French court. Instead he turned to heroic poetry, and in 1657 wrote an epic entitled *Clovis, ou la France chrestienne*, which dealt with

de la conqueste de la France, de l'establissement du Christianisme en la plus noble Monarchie qui soit maintenant au Monde, & de donner vn grand Roy & ses Successeurs pour protecteurs à l'Eglise.[57]

Tragicomedy led to epic, and historico-political epic was in turn superseded by religious epic. Aesthetically as well as ideologically speaking, the career of Desmarets career was foreseeable, and testified not only to the development of an author faced with the consequences of his choice of subject matter and but also to the greater spiritual engagement of a Christian after his 'conversion'.

NOTES

1. Margaret M. McGowan, *L'Art du ballet de cour en France (1581–1643)* (Paris: Editions du CNRS, 1963).
2. The well-known simile, *Ut pictura poesis* (literally 'as is painting, so is poetry'), from Horace's *Ars poetica*, or *Epistle to the Pisos* (l. 361), asserts the similarity or comparability of the literary and the visual arts.
3. Claude-François Ménestrier, *Le Temple de la Sagesse* (Lyon: P. Guillimin, 1663), p. 17.
4. Guillaume Colletet, *Le Grand Ballet des effets de la nature*, in *Ballets et mascarades de cour*, ed. by Paul Lacroix (1868) (Geneva: Slatkine reprints, 1968), IV, p. 191.
5. Ibid.
6. Ménestrier, *Des ballets anciens et modernes* (Paris: René Guichard, 1682), p. 18.
7. Michel de Pure, *Idée des spectacles anciens et nouveaux* (Paris: Michel Brunet, 1668), p. 214.
8. De Pure, *Idée des spectacles*, p. 210.
9. Ménestrier, *Remarques pour la conduite des ballets*, first published in *L'Autel de Lyon, Consacré à Louys Auguste* (Lyon: Jean Moulin, 1658), and reproduced in Marie-Françoise Christout, *Le Ballet de cour de Louis XIV (1643–1672). Mises en scène* (Paris: Picard, 1967), p. 223.
10. Ménestrier, *Remarques*, p. 221 ('Ceux, qui veulent, que la conduite des Ballets, soit semblable à celle des pieces de Théatre n'en connoissent pas les differences').
11. The three unities were: the unity of action, the unity of time, and the unity of space. However there was a fourth, largely unspoken, unity, that of tone, which, for almost two centuries, prevented the mixing of tragic and comic on the French stage.
12. Ménestrier, *Remarques*, p. 221.
13. See *Les Visionnaires* (Paris: Henry le Gras, 1640), Act II, scene 4, pp. 28–31.
14. *Ballet de la Prospérité des Armes de France*, in *Ballets et mascarades de cour*, VI, p. 34.
15. The three-part structure was also characteristic of opera. See Ménestrier, *Des ballets*, p. 268. In addition both the terminology and the structure used in the *Ballet de la Félicité* reflected current usage for court entertainments.
16. Aristotle, *Poetics*, in *Aristotle/Horace/Longinus. Classical Literary Criticism*, tr. by T. S. Dorsch (London: Penguin Books, 1965), chap. VII, p. 41.
17. Horace had asked in his *Ars poetica* (ll. 191–2) that '[the play] should not be either shorter or longer than five acts' (in *Classical Literary Criticism*, p. 85).
18. Ménestrier, *Remarques*, p. 225. See also Abbé Michel de Marolles, *Mémoires* (Paris: Antoine de Sommaville, 1656), II, p. 169.

19. De Pure, *Idée des spectacles*, p. 232.

20. Respectively 8, 10, 9 scenes, and 7, 9, 7, 7, 6 scenes.

21. Ménestrier, *Des ballets*, préface, n.p.

22. De Pure, *Idée des spectacles*, p. 241.

23. De Pure, *Idée des spectacles*, p. 235.

24. De Pure, *Idée des spectacles*, p. 242.

25. Ménestrier, *Des ballets*, préface, n.p. Marolles also thought that 'Ce Ballet, auec toutes ses machines & toute sa magnificence, ne fut pourtant pas vne chose si rauissante qu'on se le pourroit imaginer; parce que l'inuention n'en fut pas exactement suiuie, & que les habits & les actions de plusieurs danceurs ne se trouuerent pas assez conuenables au suiet' (*Mémoires*, I, p. 127).

26. Ménestrier described them 'comme un argument du sujet composé en vers, qui se chantent par la musique au commencement de chaque partie, ou qui se recitent' (*Remarques*, p. 225).

27. François Hédelin, Abbé d'Aubignac, *La Pratique du théâtre*, ed. by Pierre Martino (Geneva: Slatkine reprints, 1996), p. 166.

28. D'Aubignac, *La Pratique du théâtre*, p. 180.

29. *Ballet de la Prospérité des Armes de France*, [in] *Ballets et mascarades de cour*, VI, p. 33.

30. Jules de La Mesnardière, *La Poëtique* (1640) (Geneva: Slatine reprints, 1972), p. 17.

31. Ménestrier, *Des ballets*, p. 291.

32. Aristotle, *Poetics*, chap. XIII, p. 48.

33. Defined by Aristotle as 'a change from one state of affairs to its opposite, one which conforms [...] to probability or necessity' (*Poetics*, chap. XI, p. 46).

34. *Ballet de la Félicité*, [in] *Ballets et mascarades de cour*, V, p. 230.

35. Used in the plural, the *péripéties* represent oscillations of the plot, and therefore are to be distinguished from the single peripety, or reversal of fortune, which is a characteristic of the denouement.

36. They were the emblems respectively of Spain and the Holy Roman Empire.

37. La Mesnardière, *La Poëtique*, p. 7.

38. D'Aubignac, *La Pratique du théâtre*, p. 148.

39. Desmarets de Saint-Sorlin, Aux lecteurs, *Scipion. Tragi-comedie* (Paris: Henry le Gras, 1639, n.p.

40. Desmarets de Saint-Sorlin, *Les Visionnaires*, II. 4, p. 30.

41. Georges de Scudéry, Au lecteur, *Andromire* (Paris: Antoine de Sommaville, 1641), n.p.

42. Anon., *Discours à Cliton*, ed by François Lasserre (Tübingen: Biblio 17, 2000), p. 305. The example given is precisely the alternate representation on stage of Paris and Constantinople.

43. *Discours à Cliton*, p. 305.

44. *Discours à Cliton*, p. 307.

45. *Ballet de la Prospérité des Armes de France*, p. 33.

46. Jean de Schélandre, Préface au lecteur (by Ogier), *Tyr et Sidon* (Paris, Robert Estienne, 1628), n.p.

47. *Ibid.*

48. As Ménestrier noted, 'Le Ballet est un mélange de personnes graves & enjoüées, historiques & fabuleuses, naturelles & allegoriques' (*Des ballets*, p. 291). It was precisely this *mélange* which led Plautus to refer to his comedy *Amphitryon* as a *tragicomoedia*, a term which he purposely coined to describe the presence of gods, princes and servants in his play, and the resulting 'caractere meslé de diverses personnes, & de divers rôles, dont il faut que les moeurs, les sentimens, & les expressions soient diverses' (*Des ballets*, p. 288).

49. 'Pour estre beau, il faut [...] quelles [les entrées] soient si bien appropriees, que s'il y a du serieux & du Grotesque, l'on n'en voye pas deux Grotesques de suite, s'il se peut quelles soient meslées parmy les serieuses, elles en seront bien plus diuertisantes & l'on aura plus de loisir d'admirer les vnes & de rire des autres' (*La Maniere de composer et faire reussir les ballets* (Paris, 1641) (Geneva: Editions Minkoff, 1993), p. 7).

50. Ogier, préface, p. ãiiij.

51. I refer here to Stephen Orgel, *The Illusion of Power: Political Theater in the English Renaissance*

(Berkeley CA, 1975).

52. Desmarets de Saint-Sorlin, *Mirame, Tragi-Comedie. Ouuerture du Theatre de la Grande Salle du Palais Cardinal* (Paris: Henry le Gras, 1642), pp. 3–5.

53. According to Gaston H. Hall, the text of the prologue tends to suggest that ballet entries and machinery had originally been planned, although none were actually used on the day, Richelieu's illness and absence having no doubt contributed to the rather low key performance of the work at the Palais Cardinal on 17/18 November 1641 ('*Europe*, allégorie théâtrale de propagande politique', in *L'Age d'or du mécénat*, ed. by Roland Mousnier and Jean Mesnard (Paris, CNRS, 1985), pp. 319–27).

54. D'Aubignac, *La Pratique du théâtre*, p. 153.

55. *Discours à Cliton*, p. 311.

56. Aristotle, *Poetics*, chap. XXIV, p. 67. Admittedly Aristotle opposes tragedy and epic.

57. Desmarets de Saint-Sorlin, Advis, *Clovis, ou la France Chrestienne. Poeme hëroique* (Paris: Augustin Courbé & Henry le Gras, 1657), p. ẽiijv°.

Jean II Berain's Costume Designs for the Ballet *Les Plaisirs de la Paix* (1715)

JÉRÔME DE LA GORCE

In the late seventeenth century, the Swedish ambassador and architect Nicodemus Tessin the Younger used his sojourn in Paris to frequent the opera house and to build up collections of theatre designs which are now housed in the Nationalmuseum in Stockholm. He developed links with French artists and, in particular, with the Berain dynasty encouraging his son to continue the association. The son eagerly followed his advice compiling an inventory of the theatrical designs which his father had collected, an inventory which serves to identify those costume drawings for the Ballet Les Plaisirs de la Paix (1715) which are analysed in this essay and published here for the first time.

The rich collections of seventeenth- and eighteenth-century French drawings, now preserved in the Nationalmuseum in Stockholm, were built up by the celebrated architect Nicodemus Tessin, the Younger. The taste of this exceptional man extended across many domains; and he had brought from Paris (often through the good offices of his fellow compatriot Daniel Cronström) a quantity of designs showing the astonishing richness of artistic activity in Paris during the reign of Louis XIV.[1] Very early on, Tessin had interested himself in the work of Jean Berain, *Desinateur de la Chambre et du Cabinet du roi*; he had met the artist in Paris in 1687 and, until the end of his life, he held him in great esteem. From this fecund and universal genius he wanted to secure not only designs for ceilings, furniture, tapestries, carriages and tableware, but also to get hold of all the ideas Berain had planned for the operas put on in the Palais Royal at the heart of the capital. And after the death of this costume and stage designer in 1711, he made it his business to gain familiarity with the work of his successor in the lyric theatre of Paris, Jean II Berain.

After his death in 1728, his son – Carl Gustaf Tessin – concerned himself with his collection: two years later, he compiled an inventory of the designs and drawings which his father had accumulated over the years.[2] In the long list written in French, he strove to identify these works. Among the 84 sheets showing 'habits de théâtre' [theatre costumes], he specified ten drawings as follows:

> 4 Dancers (2 male, 2 female) from the opera *Les Fêtes de Thalie*
> 2 Pilgrims (1 male, 1 female) from the same opera
> 1 Dutchman from the same opera
> 3 Polish characters (1 male, 2 female) from the same opera[3]

The reference to the *Fêtes de Thalie* is somewhat surprising, for it is the only indication given by Carl Gustaf to an opera, and the details do not correspond to the designs themselves. One can search in vain for Dutchmen and Poles, or for Pilgrims in the libretto for the *Fêtes de Thalie*, yet they are found in the collection of drawings.[4] How did Carl Gustaf make such an error?

The solution can be found in the biography of Carl Gustaf Tessin. In 1714, at the very moment when the *Fêtes de Thalie* were being performed at the Palais Royal, the son of the celebrated architect was sent to Paris to finish his education. Among the many instructions which the fond father wrote down in two *mémoires*, he counselled his son to attend the Opera as an excellent means of relaxation suitable for a nineteen year old, but also in order to find out how the shows were put on; the father wrote: 'Do not forget to go to those places where the décor and costumes for opera are made, because there one learns many things.'[5] Nicodemus Tessin also asked that his son should – if possible – find drawings of the king made by such masters as Le Brun and Berain taking great care – when the works were sketched by hand – to buy them and preserve them with his own belongings. The importance of originals to enhance an already rich collection of drawings did not, however, exclude copies. On the subject of *Télémaque*, for instance, a *tragédie en musique* composed by André Cardinal Destouches and premiered in Paris on 29 November 1714, Nicodemus sought to have the décor and costumes copied: 'what is this opera Télémaque?', he asked; 'who did the designs, and are they worthy of reproduction or not? Was the scenery beautiful? And, as for the costumes of the dancers, they must be scrutinised and copied, taking care to indicate colours according to their blasonic form and to avoid putting one colour upon another and piling up metal upon metal'.[6]

A Swede – Carl Palmcrans, a reputed draftsman[7] – had accompanied Carl Gustaf to Paris, and he undertook to make copies of the décor.[8] On receipt of this news, Nicodemus expressed his deep satisfaction: 'I'm delighted that Monsieur Palmcrans has copied the sets for *Télémaque*; are they not by the son of the late Monsieur Berain?'[9]

At this date, Jean II Berain had indeed succeeded his father in designing for the lyric theatre in Paris. Even if Claude Gillot invented the décor and costumes for some productions,[10] Jean II – like his distinguished predecessor – continued to be in official control,[11] and it was to him that Nicodemus directed his son for the completion of his artistic education. He wrote to Carl Gustaf on 18 May 1715: 'I'm absolutely delighted that you are learning to draw with Monsieur Berain. May God grant that it is with firm dedication.'[12] Since his arrival in Paris in the early days of October 1714, Carl Gustaf Tessin scarcely led a studious life. To console him on the death of his mother (late 1714), Cronström strove to 'smoother his sadness' as best he could,[13] but recognising that his charge was in want of some occupation, along with his tutor Weslander, he encouraged him to try his hand at art and to go – every afternoon – 'to draw with Monsieur Berain'.[14]

These biographical details make it clear that many of the costume drawings conserved at Stockholm and described in the 1730 inventory as 'coloured by the hand of Berain', were acquired by Carl Gustaf direct from the artist; indeed, the purchaser wrote 'although 10 *livres* each was paid for them, they are only valued at 5 *livres*'.[15] The circumstances surrounding their purchase, and at a time when Jean II Berain (at the beginning of his career) could benefit from the reputation of his illustrious father, doubtless justified the reduction in price. They also explain the initial error in identifying the drawings. In May 1715, when Carl Gustaf was attending Berain's studio, neither the *Fêtes de Thalie* nor *Télémaque* were in production at the Palais Royal; another work was being performed there – *Les Plaisirs de la Paix* [The Pleasures of Peace]. This spectacle, premiered on 29 April, displayed all the dancers found in the Stockholm archives: in addition to the Pilgrims, the Dutchman and the Poles, one may also recognise the Germans and the Shepherds who performed the first two entries of the opera-ballet. Many reasons explain Carl Gustaf's original confusion: the opera-ballets were produced on the same stage, one after the other, in the same period, and the undoubted success of the *Fêtes de Thalie*, put on again for three months from 12 March 1715, eclipsed all memory of *Les Plaisirs*.[16]

Les Plaisirs de la Paix, set to music by Thomas-Louis Bourgeois to a libretto composed by Menesson, had little success, despite the faithful reflection of everyday life in the first three entries, and despite the prevailing taste for local colour and for the comic masks introduced in the last interlude. The brothers Parfaict, in their theatre dictionary, noting that the ballet never re-appeared on stage helped to contribute to its permanent demise.[17] And yet, as the composer had done in 1713 with *Les Amours déguisés*, he took part in the interpretation as a singer.[18] Menesson must bear responsibility for the failure. According to the brothers Parfaict, the librettist did not enjoy a good reputation: although he was an honourable man and thought he had sufficient talent to compose opera lyrics, not one of his works was successful.[19]

However, the theme of *Les Plaisirs de la Paix* was topical; it celebrated the return of peace after a long period of war in Europe, confirmed by the treatises of Utrecht and Rastadt. In a preface, Menesson explained his intention:

This ballet is an allegory of peace and it is easy to see the connections. Winter represents the tranquillity that has descended over Europe and Venus the harmony re-established between nations. The Cyclops represent the Arts, Bacchus and Comus – abundance. Momus and Carnival bring forth pleasures and entertainments.[20]

In addition to the diversity of characters chosen to represent his ideas of the ballet and which appeared independently throughout the opera, Menesson – wishing to retain a tight structure appropriate to dramatic forms – introduced a certain homogeneity by the use of interludes which served as a kind of transition between each part; he explained, 'although each entry has its own subject, care has been taken to link them through interludes so that play and prologue constitute a single subject'. This concern to stress unity is underlined by the way in which successive decors appear, one after the other, during the action – an unusual procedure, as Menesson clarified:

The action takes place in Winter's Palace, that is to say in the Domain of Tranquillity, and all the changes of scene which take place against the back of the stage are no more than ornaments, mere decorations introduced by the different festivities desired by the gods.[21]

The libretto itself distributed before the performance confirms that, apart from the last interlude for which the entire stage machinery was transformed, there were few changes of scene after the prologue, Winter's Palace serving for the prologue and subsequent entries with minor adjustments only to the back cloth.[22] In the first scene, the snow-covered landscape which spectators perceived through a vestibule remained in place throughout the performance, while a salon was depicted at the front of the stage with trophies and balconies. In scene four, persons of different nations occupied the balconies, having come to observe the ballet entries performed on the floor of the stage. While some performers danced, others sang, and together they constituted the *fête galante*[23] which Venus had announced in the prologue as a celebration of the return of peace.

So, nations were reconciled; and Germans, Poles, Swiss, Italians and one French lady were chosen to demonstrate their rejoicing at the coming of a period favourable to their amorous affairs. Several drawings by Jean II Berain give an idea of how these Europeans appeared to the public. One couple, described as dancers (male and female) can be identified as Germans when one examines carefully the decorated headdress of the lady dancer (see Figure 1).[24] The small box hat, decorated with feathers, the ruff whose whiteness reaches down into her *décolleté* bordered with black velvet, all these features were reminiscent of the style adopted in the Rhine valley during the Renaissance; in a volume of engraved costume designs, still preserved in the Bibliothèque nationale de France (BNF), one can find her model inscribed thus: 'honest lady from Strasbourg'.[25] Until the beginning of the eighteenth century, Alsace – despite its close association with France – was closely aligned to German culture. For the German male dancer, Jean II Berain adapted his design (see Figure 2)[26] to the model of the lady; in addition to the headdress and ruff, the same common elements decorated the sleeves, covered with a longer over-sleeve on which striped motifs were stitched.

The Poles were characterised by their hair styles and rich turbans reminiscent of the Orient, evoking – in the two ladies – a proximity with Asia (see Figures 3 and 4),[27] while the male dancer (or singer) carried sabre and shield and wore a hat whose edges were lined with fur (see Figure 5).[28] The cold climes of winter from which these people came are evoked by the fur-lined garments which they all wore. Their habits are also festooned with sumptuous ornaments, with natural and flower motifs and, around the buttonholes are frogged designs with elaborate trimmings intended to enhance the effect of richness. All these details could have been borrowed by Jean II Berain from the engravings showing the Polish military and gentlemen from the king's guard, models which circulated freely in the seventeenth century.[29] In contrast to the designs for Germans, the artist used the male model as the pattern for his Polish ladies where the influence of contemporary fashion is particularly visible.

As far as the drawing for the costume of the Dutch is concerned (see

Fig. 1. Jean II Berain, costume design for a German (female), Stockholm, Nationalmuseum.

Fig. 2. Jean II Berain, costume design for a German (male), Stockholm, Nationalmuseum.

Fig. 3. Jean II Berain, costume design for a Pole (female), Stockholm, Nationalmuseum.

Fig. 4. Jean II Berain, costume design for another Pole (female), Stockholm, Nationalmuseum.

Fig. 5. Jean II Berain, costume design for a Pole (male), Stockholm, Nationalmuseum.

Figure 6)[30] (for which there is no female equivalent), Jean II Berain carefully avoided playing up to contemporary taste. The conception can be fully
appreciated as we have an original drawing annotated by the artist himself (see
Figure 7).[31] The tall hat, style Henri IV, is made of felt and is the colour of fallen
leaves, topped by red feathers and a blue band bordered in silver. Beneath the
collar which frames the face, the yellow doublet is close-fitting (termed a 'corset')
and, like the sleeve and wide breeches with their cross-braiding, recalled the style
Louis XIII. The doublet support is edged out in bluish silver ribbon, a colour
picked out again on the sleeves and in the lining of the red cape.

For the Shepherds' costumes (see Figures 8 and 10),[32] there are also drawings annotated by Jean II Berain (see Figures 9 and 11).[33] These performers
danced on stage in scenes 7 and 8 to the sound of pipes all ready to celebrate the
union of Timante and Iris whose ceremony formed part of Bacchus' festival.
After a woodland scene, the back cloth had changed to reveal a trelliss beneath
which creatures crowned with vine leaves were enjoying their wine.[34] It is within
this pastoral setting that shepherds danced and sang uniting the pleasures of the
table to those of love. In contrast to the depiction of national costumes, Jean II
Berain leaves no doubt as to the role of these figures; their attitudes shown in the
drawings make clear that they formed part of the *corps de ballet*. To characterise
them, the artist has perpetuated stylistic features well-known from his father's
work: elegant but slightly old-fashioned headdresses and wide slashed sleeves.[35]
Yet these echos of fashions from the past, intended to evoke a certain rusticity of
manner, in no way detract from the extreme refinement of the costumes as can
be seen from the artist's own comments on the detail of his drawings (see Figures
9 and 11). The two blue-coloured costumes are delicately picked out in red,
touched in on the feathers and on the undergarments of the dancer, and on the
ornaments decorating the wide skirt, while hints of blue are kept for the tunic
and stockings. Fringes and silver edging, designed to make a splash, are provided
so that they might sparkle on stage and under the lights.

Although Shepherds occurred frequently in the lyric theatre repertoire,
Pilgrims are encountered less often. Their presence here, however, is of particular interest since they appear in many of Antoine Watteau's works at this
period: in the famous l'*Ile de Cythère* [Island of Cythera], *Pilgrimage to the Ile de
Cythère*, and *Departure for Cythère*. Historians have pointed out the links between
these works and the Ballet *Les Amours déguisés* (August, 1713) whose prologue
opens with the perspective of a port and a flotilla of cupids setting out for *Cythère*,
and where Venus herself appears 'in the company of Pleasures & Games, dis-
guised as sailors'.[36] Although Pilgrims did not figure in the *Amours déguisés* (1713),
they are prominent in the *Plaisirs de la Paix* (1715), dancing in a 'special place
prepared for a mascarade' where Carnival appears and banishes all troubles,
sadness and grief with his playful attention to the affairs of love,[37] and introducing
a divertissement accompanied by choirs exalting the power of Pleasures filled
with charm. The dancers depicted in two drawings by Jean II Berain (see Figures
12 and 13)[38] figured in a 'ballet général', celebrating pleasure and bringing the
spectacle to an end with much panache.

Fig. 6. Jean II Berain, costume design for a Dutchman, Stockholm, Nationalmuseum.

Fig. 7. Jean II Berain, costume design for the same Dutchman, annotated by the artist, Stockholm, Nationalmuseum.

Fig. 8. Jean II Berain, costume design for a shepherd, Stockholm, Nationalmuseum.

Fig. 9. Jean II Berain, costume design for the same shepherd, annotated by the artist,
Stockholm, Nationalmuseum.

Fig. 10. Jean II Berain, costume design for a shepherdess, Stockholm, Nationalmuseum.

Fig. 11. Jean II Berain, costume design for the same shepherdess, annotated by the artist, Stockholm, Nationalmuseum.

Fig. 12. Jean II Berain, costume design for a Pilgrim (male), Stockholm, Nationalmuseum.

Fig. 13. Jean II Berain, costume design for a Pilgrim (female), Stockholm, Nationalmuseum.

It is somewhat surprising that Menesson refers to 'comic masks' alongside more serious characters.[39] Apart from the pears which hang from the staffs of the Pilgrims neither in their attitude nor in their accoutrements (as drawn by Jean II Berain) suggest any comic designation. Like the figures in Watteau's paintings they are more akin to gallantry. And as shepherds in the opera, they hold staffs in their hands decorated with ribbons as if they were crooks, while the substantial purse which the lady Pilgrim carries across her person is reminiscent of a game bag. If one compares their outfits to those represented by Watteau or Bernard Picard where scallop shells frequently hang from the shepherds' staffs, here – in an effort to make clear their pilgrim status[40] – scallops appear everywhere: on the headdress and capes, and around the base of the tunic.

In this way Jean II Berain sought to respect the decorum observed by his father and by Gissey, making sure that his characters were properly equipped to appear on stage. The sung verses of the opera were not always easy to understand and the artist was required to make sure that the audience comprehended the action. Thus, the drawings in the Tessin collection, which are here identified as belonging to *Les Plaisirs de la Paix* (1715), not only confirm opera/ballet traditions, they also allow us to understand better an artist hitherto somewhat neglected, and (thanks to the richness of the collection) to appreciate his working habits and value their qualities.

And yet, despite the natural attribution of this material to the hand of Jean II Berain, his actual contribution is not easy to establish because of the diversity of techniques used. According to Carl Gustaf Tessin who knew him well, the sketches which he obtained from the Berain studio were 'coloured in' by the artist himself – an habitual tactic to ensure that the products were more attractive to amateur buyers. No document affirms his authorship of the black chalk or pen and black ink drawings.

The same questions arise when one considers his other projects, similarly coloured and accompanied by annotations for the attention of artisans, and where several hands seem involved. What role did his studio and his assistants play in their production? Can one attribute to the artist himself the most accomplished of the drawings such as the one he annotated for the shepherd (see Figure 9)?

Although there are many unknowns, the identification of many drawings for the costumes of *Les Plaisirs de la Paix* (1715) should encourage further research on Jean II Berain and lead to a better understanding of the repertoire whose iconographical sources have been little studied. For the history of the theatre and of art, the last years of Louis XIV's reign and the beginning of the Regency are exciting since not all their secrets have yet been revealed. What do we know about the productions which revealed Chinese or Japanese décors and the appearance in the theatres of Paris of *rocaille* taste? With the discovery of the Stockholm drawings, we have gained greater appreciation of the diversity of characters created for opera and ballet, especially the Pilgrims mentioned above, which were completely new to the public; and it is impossible to believe that Watteau and other artists of his time were unaware of their existence.

NOTES

1. On this subject, see Roger-Armand Weigert and Carl Hernmarck, *L'Art en France et en Suède (1693–1718), extraits d'une correspondance entre l'architecte Nicodème Tessin le jeune et Daniel Cronström* (Stockholm, 1964).

2. Begun in 1730, Nationalmuseum, Konstnärsarkivet, Biografica samlingen; See Martin Olin's introduction to *Nicodème Tessin the Younger, Sources, Works, Collections: Architectural Drawings I (Ecclesiastical and Garden Architecture)*, (Stockholm, 2004), pp. 9–32.

3. Manuscript inventory, p. 31.

4. Stockholm, Nationalmuseum, THC 1427, 1429, 1430, 1432, 1433, 1440, 1441, 1442, 1443 and 1444.

5. Stockholm, Riksarkivet, E 5717.

6. Ibid.

7. According to a letter from Nicodemus (21 April/ 1 May, 1714) published in *L'Art en France et en Suède*, op. cit., p. 378.

8. A copy showing the décor for the second act of *Télémaque* is preserved in the Nationalmuseum. It has been published in La Gorce, *Berain, dessinateur du Roi-Soleil* (Paris, 1986), pp. 140 and 142.

9. Stockholm, Riksarkivet, E 5717.

10. On Gillot's work for the opera, see La Gorce, *Fééries d'opéra: décors, machines et costumes en France (1645–1765)*, (Paris, 1997), p. 20.

11. Jean II Berain's career is examined by Roger-Armand Weigert in his study of the father, *Jean I Berain, Dessinateur de la Chambre et du Cabinet du roi (1640–1711)*, (Paris, 1937), I, pp. 133–61.

12. Stockholm, Riksarkivet, E 5717.

13. Letter dated 23 January 1715; Stockholm, Riksarkivet, E 5717.

14. Letter dated 26 May 1715, published in *L'Art en France et en Suède*, op. cit., p. 386.

15. Inventory, p. 31.

16. For a chronology of operas performed at this time, see La Gorce, *L'Opéra à Paris au temps de Louis XIV: histoire d'un théâtre* (Paris, 1992), pp. 197–203.

17. François et Claude Parfaict, *Dictionnaire des théâtres de Paris* (Paris, 1767), IV, p. 55.

18. Menesson, *Les Plaisirs de la Paix, ballet représenté pour la première fois par l'Académie royale de musique, le Lundi vingt-neuvième avril 1715* (Paris, chez Pierre Ribou, 1715), p. iv.

19. Bibliothèque nationale de France, Manuscrits fr., nouvelles acquisitions 6532, II, p. 4.

20. Menesson, op. cit., 'Avertissement', non-paginated.

21. Ibid.

22. *Les Plaisirs de la Paix, Ballet, mis en musique par Mr Bourgeois, ci-devant Maître de Musique des Cathédrales de Toul et Strasbourg* (Paris, chez Ribou, 1715).

23. Menesson, op. cit., pp. xii and 7.

24. Stockholm, Nationalmuseum, THC 1443 (black chalk, pen and black ink drawing with some water colouring, h. 278 × l. 202 mm).

25. BNF, Estampes Ob, 14a, pl. 10. I would like to thank Madeleine de Terris (Cabinet des Estampes) for her help in tracing the engraved series of peoples of Europe.

26. Stockholm, Nationalmuseum, THC 1444 (black chalk, pen and black ink drawing with some water colouring, h. 278 × l. 201 mm).

27. Stockholm, Nationalmuseum, THC 1433 (black chalk, pen and black ink drawing with some water colouring, h. 325 × l. 238 mm) and THC 1440 (also black chalk, pen and black ink drawing with some water colouring, h. 322 × l. 233 mm). Another example of this last drawing can be found in New York (The Pierpont Morgan Library, 1982.75, f. 31).

28. Stockholm, Nationalmuseum, THC 1432 (black chalk, pen and black ink drawing with some water colouring, h. 378 × l. 252 mm).

29. See the engravings of Polish costumes, BNF, Estampes Ob 128 fol and Ob 130 pet.fol.

30. Stockholm, Nationalmuseum, THC 1427 (black chalk, pen and black ink drawing with some water colouring, h. 378 × l. 236 mm).

31. Stockholm, Nationalmuseum, K.16, f.169 (black chalk drawing with some water colouring, h. 426 × l. 678 mm).

32. Stockholm, Nationalmuseum, THC 1441 and 1442 (black chalk, pen and black ink drawings with some water colouring, h. 278 × l. 202 mm).
33. Stockholm, Nationalmuseum, K.2, f. 97 and 107 (black chalk drawings, h. 536 × l. 398 mm).
34. Menesson, op. cit., pp. 16, 27–8.
35. On this topic, see *Fééries d'opéra*, op. cit., no. 133, pp. 130–1.
36. Louis Fuzelier, *Les Amours déguisez, ballet, représenté pour la première fois par l'Académie royale de musique, le Mardi vingt-deuxième août 1713* (Paris, chez Pierre Ribou, 1713), p. 1. On the subject of the *Ile de Cythère* and its use by Watteau and in the theatre of the period, see François Moureau, 'Watteau dans son temps', in the Exhibition catalogue *Watteau 1684–1721* (Paris, 1984), pp. 495–503; and Georgia Cowart, 'Watteau's *Pilgrimage to Cythera* and the Subversive Utopia of the Opera-Ballet', *Art Bulletin*, LXXXIII/3 (September 2001), 461–78.
37. Menesson, op. cit., p. 43.
38. Stockholm, Nationalmuseum, THC 1429 and 1430 (black chalk, pen and black ink drawings with some water colouring, h. 278 × l. 202 mm, h. 318 × l. 235 mm).
39. Menesson, op. cit., p. iii.
40. For the depiction of pilgrims at this period, see Moureau, op. cit, p. 524, 'Iconographie théâtrâle'.

Into the Labyrinth: Kenneth MacMillan and his Ballets

CLEMENT CRISP

This study explores the choreographic themes and the emotional and psychic concerns which are so central to the creativity of Kenneth MacMillan. Clement Crisp, who has seen and reviewed MacMillan's ballets for forty years, from the earliest apprentice works to the final Judas Tree, offers some observations on the nature of MacMillan's inspiration, on the ideas that fired his imagination and their realisation in dance.

'A word is not the same with one writer as with another: one tears it from his guts; the other pulls it out of his overcoat pocket.' So said Charles Péguy, and the comment is no less appropriate when considering choreographers. There are the 'overcoat pocket' dance-makers, in many styles, whose essential superficiality, whose repetitions of effects, reduce their work to formula rather than creativity. The same tricks, the same abrasive attitudes, crass re-visitings of old ballets or the same angry obsessions, come round with dire regularity, like the hands on a clock. Audiences, happy to recognise yet again something they have recognised before, applaud, and critical comment – no less reassured by the familiar – will make capital about an imagined 'style' and the supposed 'language' of the creator, when what is most notable is the timorous nature of the creativity, its complacency and lack of self-awareness, its reluctance to dare. Labels are written and stuck on, and the dance-maker is neatly and conveniently identified for posterity – or at least for the publicity machine of his company.

Kenneth MacMillan was not of this kind. His ballets came from his guts. Throughout his career, his psyche worried and fretted at his undeniable and considerable talent, goading him into producing dances. His means of coping with his own emotional stresses was sometimes to exorcise them by making ballets, but these were both therapy and not-therapy for him. His talent was too uncompromising to allow him the ultimate self-indulgence of the stage as confessional or analyst's couch. He made ballets because he had to, in order to assuage his daemon, which was the daemon that lies within a true creator in whatever artistic discipline and must speak through the artist's work, and because he was a choreographer associated with a great national company, his ballets governed by its exigencies (he knew these as director and as chief choreographer), whose dancers and whose artistic history made demands which he understood and honoured.

I knew MacMillan. As a critic I knew his work from the first apprentice piece, *Somnambulism*, in 1953, to the final *Judas Tree* nearly forty years later. Our friendship sprang from my admiration for his ballets, and from the advocacy for the merits of his choreography which he read in *The Financial Times*, an advocacy initiated by Andrew Porter, when he was both music and dance critic for that paper from the inception of its arts pages, which came just as MacMillan's creative career began, and continued by me when I joined the F.T. There was only one rule, unspoken yet mutually understood: we never discussed MacMillan's ballets before their arrival on stage, and we rarely discussed them afterwards. My reviews in *The Financial Times* were thus, I made sure, un-corrupted by prior information. I admired MacMillan's great gift as a dance-maker, and was fascinated and rewarded by his power to explore the human psyche and to find acute physical imagery to convey his understanding of the emotional subterfuges, those twists and evasions of feeling, that fed the theatrical life of his characters.

In many ways he became, as I have noted before, a psycho-analyst to them, letting them voice their terrors, desires, anguish, in movement that pushed academic dance far beyond the then existing limits of the *danse d'école*. On occasion he drove his characters into corners, forcing them to an ultimate expression of their feeling. In so doing, he guided and goaded ballet towards a vocabulary of rare expressionistic force, but one still underpinned by his own belief in the rule of academic form and discipline. At his most piercing, he gave movement a scalding veracity, finding shapes and sequences of dance and pose which were dragged from deep in the subconscious of his characters and, I am inclined to believe, of himself. Occasionally, he did not at first comprehend why his creatures moved thus. He only knew that this was the way in which they *must* move and be seen: reason, experience, would later explain initial feeling and reaction, both on his part and on theirs. He once, uncharacteristically but revealingly, said to me: 'Sometimes it takes three or four performances of one of my ballets for me to understand why a character moves in a particular way.' This suggests something of the procedures of psycho-analysis where, only after prolonged self-enquiry, may the patient understand the underlying motive for an action or a feeling. The journey into the labyrinths of the mind can be long, tortuous.

MacMillan's imaginative sensitivity in shaping his characters' physical behaviour can clearly be seen in the duet in his *Isadora* of 1981, when Duncan learns of the death of her children, and turns to Paris Singer (father of her son; Gordon Craig was the father of her daughter) in an anguished avowal of grief. The rawness of their shared despair, and also the phenomenal outlines of the movement (Isadora and Singer falling and almost squatting in the depth of their sorrow) partake of the force of Picasso's brush-strokes in *Guernica*. I sensed that beyond this expressive point academic choreography could not go. That audiences were profoundly moved by this harsh, beautifully ugly exposition of grief, and responded to the drama of its imagery, cannot be doubted, even in a ballet as diffuse and as flawed in structure as this *Isadora*.

In another provocative work, *Valley of Shadows*, MacMillan again sought to show the darkest aspects of life, by proposing scenes set in a concentration camp. His portrayal of Jewish victims of this abomination was direct in its austerity, and essential to a dramatic ballet concerned with evasions of social fact. But the Royal Ballet repertory, so richly endowed with fairies and sunny peasants and genteel, if suffering, heroines, could not sustain such an assault on its sensibilities: *Valley of Shadows* disappeared from the stage.

MacMillan's choreography enabled him to look at certain of his own ghosts. A shadowed childhood, which Jann Parry's new biography of MacMillan makes clear through her elucidations of his anxieties – and the versions of these which he would later offer to the world – and his escape from it (and from his family) through balletic training and eventually through balletic creativity, would always mark his introspective character. Even in his earliest works there is an un-mistakable concern with the mind, with its wounds and its means of dealing with those wounds, sometimes hiding them from public gaze, suffering their hurt in private. His first apprentice essay for the Sadler's Wells Choreographic Group was *Somnambulism*, where dreams spoke of the sleep-walker's un-masked identity. In *Laiderette*, which he made a year later, happiness in love is destroyed by a secret revealed – the baldness of the Pierrot-girl heroine. Two years later, in *Noctambules*, his first ballet for the Covent Garden troupe, a hypnotist forces four characters to expose their desires and their fears. MacMillan as analyst to his dance characters is shadowed by MacMillan as a creator already feeding on his anxieties of spirit, a doubling of concerns which would thereafter mark several of his ballets.

It would be wrong, in thus probing into motive on the part of a creator – and of characters who can be seen as extensions of his own concerns and perhaps of his *persona* – to overlook the fact that MacMillan was a brilliant maker of dance as dance, rather than of dance-as-therapy in choreographic terms. He has, as we saw so vitally in *Danses concertantes* of 1955, which was his earliest commissioned work for the Sadler's Wells Theatre Ballet, a dazzling gift for realising music in movement. *Danses concertantes* glittered with ideas, born very much of their time and its youthful creative climate in cinema and theatre, bright-cut and innovative, secure in their academic roots but turning an accepted language into something wittily young, engagingly allusive. (Hands became butterflies or masks; arms emerged from the wings of the stage; steps bounced and flashed over the score; a hidden world of liaisons, flirtatious tension, was hinted at, yet never made explicit.) This ability to think anew about a traditional language was a constant of MacMillan's creativity, and in such later works as *The Prince of the Pagodas* or *La Fin du jour* or *Symphony* his easy manipulation of ballet's central vocabulary was a continuing delight.

But with early recognition of his talent, and the responsibilities which came with his success and his choreographic association with the Royal Ballet, there also came the desire to realise and develop his fascination with ballet's expressive potential. In 1958, *The Burrow*, with its concern about a trapped community (the linking with the world of Ann Frank is not wholly justifiable), developed his interest in dance as probe as well as expression, and brought him into a first contact with the dance gifts of Lynn Seymour, both as subtle actress and as ravishing dance-physique. It was *The Invitation*, in 1960, which best showed his early interest in exploring the ambiguous nature of sexual needs and frustration. In that same year he had provided, in a realisation of Stravinsky's *Le Baiser de la fée*, an exquisite response to a score, the choreography most happily born of the music, and set on three dancers (Svetlana Beriosova as the Fairy; Lynn Seymour as the Bride; Donald McLeary as the Young Man) whose fluency in movement, grace of manner, were ideally realised in an essentially lyrical choreography: the Mill Scene duet for the Young Man and the Bride remains one of MacMillan's loveliest creations, felicitous in showing young love, ravishing in its response to the score).

With *The Invitation* MacMillan spoke more clearly than before about the sexuality of his characters. The narrative, set in an undefined but warm-climated and Edwardian bourgeois household, tells of a boy and girl, cousins, experiencing the first pangs of affection and sexual awareness, who are seduced by an unhappily married Husband and Wife. The boy's initiation by the Wife is un-shadowed and can be seen as a rite of passage. The girl, more innocent, misunderstands the Husband's interest, responds almost childishly to him, and is raped. Her life, we are shown in her final frozen walk towards the curtain and her future, is irretrievably damaged. MacMillan's literary sources for this drama – Beatriz Guido's *The House of the Angel* and Colette's *Le Blé en herbe* – are conflated to provide a dramatic framework for dancing which speaks with subtlety about youth and experience: the boy laying his head tentatively upon the girl's breast, and repeating the gesture with the Wife, who responds with a frank acceptance of his sexual need. Throughout, the dance reveals those nuances of desire masked by social manners that marked MacMillan as a sure dramatist and as a poet of feeling.

The creative path thus discovered is one followed and broadened in MacMillan's subsequent choreographies. In *Romeo and Juliet* of 1965, in *Manon* of 1974, he produced two big theatrical machines which were demanded both by the Royal Ballet's history of developing the full-evening ballet, and by the public's taste for such elaborate spectacles. In them, he managed to delineate characters whose emotional and sexual identities were rewardingly complex. These were real people, neither constrained by balletic convention, nor two-dimensional in their emotions. Complex structure, space for the narrative and the dance and the emotional life of the characters to open out, brought both weight and density to behaviour, from the hints of Lady Capulet's passion for Tybalt to Lescaut's moral piracy. These people lived after curtain-fall. With the full-evening *Anastasia* and *Isadora* MacMillan can be seen to be straining at every accepted boundary of the old ballet, hitting out at dramatic expectation and theatrical rule, and, alas, not succeeding as he had hoped. Then, in *Mayerling*, that most layered and resonant of his big ballets, he triumphed, forcing the conventions to accept his characters, forcing ballet itself to see the full-evening creation as a means of drawing a full-length portrait of a young man denied the parental affection he craves, tormented by oedipal feelings, by sexual excess, by his historical identity as heir to a fractured double-crown. (It is ironic that *Mayerling* can be viewed as a fascinating inversion of that most popular of balletic *idées reçues*, *Swan Lake*, in its concern with love in death and a doomed Prince.) *Mayerling* offered a love-story, impossibly romanticised by writers and by cinema, which MacMillan both studies and de-glamourises.

With the one-act *Anastasia* which he had made for Lynn Seymour when they were both working in Berlin at the Staatsoper as the 1960s ended, MacMillan produced a ballet which looked with particular emphasis upon the nature of memory and of the psychosis of a 'pretender'. His Anna Anderson believes – or wants the world to believe – that she is the Grand Duchess escaped somehow from the Bolshevik massacre of the Imperial Russian family at Ekaterinburg. Lynn Seymour's prodigious interpretation, from the first tentative steps over the floorboards of a Berlin hospital by the crop-headed woman whom we first see, in quest of the faintest trace of reality, to the extraordinary figure riding round the stage on her hospital bed in something like triumphant self-realisation, was a thrilling exposition and justification of MacMillan's quest for dance as key to the psyche, and for choreography as expressive means. Against all reason, we, the audience, believed Anna Anderson's ludicrous fantasy, because MacMillan (and Seymour) were so commanding in their advocacy for the lies, so truthful in exploring Anna Anderson's mental state.

Anna Anderson's world of delusion and psychic malfunction was to find parallels in others of MacMillan's most searching creations. In 1979 he made *Playground* for the Sadler's Wells Royal Ballet, based on a score by Gordon Crosse which he had heard and liked. An initial thought about the Orpheus legend was transmuted into a narrative in which a young man 'descends' (by climbing over a wire fence which was the enclosure in which the cast were constrained – a dazzling image by Yoland Sonnabend who designed the piece) into a group of men and women who are 'playing' at being children, their ragbag of clothes, their mimicry of 'grown-ups', including this. They act out childhood fantasies: a girl (Marion Tait, piteous as the Eurydice figure whom the intruder singles out) suffers an epileptic fit, and this is an echo of MacMillan's own childhood, relating to a condition suffered by his mother, and it will feature again in his reverberant study of sibling relationships, *My Brother, My Sister*. The playing out of childhood games, the shifting and almost hallucinatory nature of identities, even the question of why the Young Man (memorably danced by Desmond Kelly) should enter this enclosed world, and the final coup of white-clad medical attendants who supervise the inmates as they return to their institutional garb and strap the Young Man in a straight-jacket, suggest how MacMillan's fascination with extreme mental states was channelled into a forceful yet compassionate dance structure. *Playground*'s shifting realities, its offering of two intertwined states to its audience – therapy as fantasy leading to self-realisation – was told in what seemed uncompromising terms, although it could be argued that even the supposed doctor-attendants were also patients in this institution. Its theatrical effects, its frank dance language, were potent, shocking, hard-edged. (MacMillan remarked to me, early on, that he would like to see it performed by the artists of Pina Bausch's Wuppertal troupe: it was truly a piece of *Tanz-theater*.)

It can be argued that in certain works MacMillan, uncharacteristically, picked on an easy target, one which so suggested 'a MacMillan ballet' in its exploration of sexual identity as to be almost self-parodistic. I felt this with his version of Strindberg's *Miss Julie*, made for Marcia Haydee in Stuttgart in 1969, which had all the necessary components of passion and social tension yet did not seem to challenge him. The bold expressionism of *Wozzeck*, which served as theme for *Different Drummer* in 1984, might also have seemed too easy a target. In the event, the staging provided a means of exploring Wozzeck's hapless condition in movement of uncompromising directness, matching the grotesque ferocity of Georg Buchner's original. And *My Brother, My Sisters*, made first for the Stuttgart Ballet in 1978, offered choreography of extreme subtlety.

I feel that this is the furthest that MacMillan journeyed in mapping the every-shifting territory of human relationships. An initial interest in the lives of the Bronte sisters and their brother was to lead on to a study of a family 'set apart by landscape and circumstance' whose five sisters are dominated by their brother, whose games are fantasies in which menace, desire, insecurity, terror, all play their part, with masks as a frightening means of evoking fear and dissolving identity. The score comprised music by Schoenberg and Webern, its sonorities perfectly matched by MacMillan's taut, night-haunted dances, with death as a terrible resolution to the action. One other character is seen, a man who walks through the piece as an observer. Listed as 'He' in the cast, he passes through the action, untouched and untouching.

A few months before his death in 1992, while his wife and daughter were in Australia, MacMillan spent a week-end at my house in the country. We talked of everything *but* ballet, save for one moment when I decided that I must know about 'He'. 'It's me, of course,' said MacMillan, and here was not simply an answer to a question, but a key to something of his creative process. His fascination and concern with the characters in his ballets was always, by the nature of his creative procedures, that of the analytical being who observes and charts the drama being played out.

My Brother, My Sisters is extraordinary in its sustained dance-mood of half-felt, half-guessed menace – rather as we can find in the novels of Shirley Jackson where the unspoken is as frightening as explicit terrors. In achieving this, MacMillan showed how surely he could grip his audience. A simple *pas de bourrée* seems like a whispered threat; a bespectacled sister, her glasses stolen, moves in blind anxiety over the stage; incestuous passion blossoms in secret smiles, revelatory gesture and dance; the brother's epileptic fit curves and threshes in imagery that turns physical anguish into gripping dance, draws the sisters, fascinated, into its fact. Throughout, this world of enclosed and secretive relationships is sustained by choreography that rarely rises above a mezzo-forte. The piece is a mastery display of creative assurance.

In one other short dance work, *Sea of Troubles*, made initially for a small dance group sprung from the Royal Ballet, MacMillan produced a gloss upon

Hamlet in which he had entire creative freedom from the constraints of working for a large national ensemble. The result was choreography where identity itself became unclear (since dancers doubled Shakespeare's characters, save for Hamlet himself). These shifts led to an extraordinary means of communicating Hamlet's own confusion of spirit. Hamlet (played with touching finesse by Michael Batchelor, a dancer of purest classic style, who died young) seemed both victim of the drama and its motive force, his life defined by the unreality of his state.

In what was to prove his final ballet, *The Judas Tree* of 1992, MacMillan produced choreography as theatrically gripping and as emotionally reverberant as any he had made before, and, I would venture, more daring in its manner. His command of effect, the bravura layering of feeling and action, the mounting tension that leads to a final crisis, and the allusive means by which the choreography signals motive and events, are exceptional in expressive power. What more brave in balletic terms than the way in which the gang-rape of the Woman is shown, and what more persuasive of despair and unease than the exhausted and repeated running circuit of the stage by the Foreman's friend, the Christ-figure, piercingly created by Michael Nunn? Transferred to a Canary Wharf building site, transmuted and yet still truthful, we find the betrayal of Christ by Judas, the multiple and unchanging identities of womankind as mother, beloved, available flesh and consoling Virgin (in a formidably truthful performance by Leanne Benjamin). Nothing is fixed or certain, as a group of labourers seem by turn gang and disciples, and murder and betrayal take place before derelict motor cars which are both hulks and tomb, and historical allusion is born of murder-thriller procedure (as the Foreman, who is Judas, draws round the body of the murdered friend who is the Christ-figure). Driven in part by his desire to create for a great dance-actor (Irek Mukhamedov), MacMillan's choreography here seems more hallucinatory in its images, its 'meaning', its enquiry into the nature of passion, of guilt, of Jungian symbols, than ever before.

With much of the MacMillan repertory, one can see how the spark of unease, the first idea of some wound to a personality, can start the choreographic fires. Throughout his creative life, MacMillan made ballets which sought to express the human condition as he saw it – in a post-Freudian age. It would, though, be wholly misleading to view his dance-making, his significance, merely in terms of psychiatric enquiry. He was, first and foremost, a man who believed in, loved, was shaped by, the *danse d'école*, the language of ballet's daily class. He used it with felicity and imaginative boldness, in extending its range in plotless creations: *The Four Seasons* was dazzlingly inventive in shaping academic steps; both *Gloria* and *Requiem* show how it may be used to face the presence of death; and in his masterly version of *Song of the Earth* – and in his *Rite of Spring* – the movement speaks with grand authority. But he was a child of his psychologically alert time, and the expressive potential of the academic dance was something that fascinated him, as it had earlier fascinated Antony Tudor and would fascinate Roland Petit, who continues to this day to make dance hugely revealing of an inner life. MacMillan's double talent – a commanding gift for movement itself; a willingness, a need, to dare in dance so that choreography might treat of character and personality as did the theatre and film of his time – has meant that ballet has learned to speak of character rather than cliché. MacMillan has, so to say, shown it the real world.

The Publications of Margaret M. McGowan

A. BOOKS AND EDITIONS

1. *L'art du Ballet de Cour en France, 1581–1643*, Paris, 1963, 351 pp.
2. *Les fêtes de cour en Savoie. L'Oeuvre de Philippe d'Aglié*, Société de l'Histoire de Théâtre, 1970, 80 pp.
3. *Montaigne's Deceits*, London, 1974, 207 pp.
4. *L'entrée de Henri II à Rouen, 1550*, Amsterdam, Theatrum Orbis Terrarum, 1974, lii + 130 pp.
5. *Balet Comique de la Reyne, 1581*, Medieval and Renaissance Texts, Binghamton, 1982, xlix + 152 pp.
6. *Form and Meaning. Aesthetic Coherence in Seventeenth-century French Drama*, ed. with Ian D. McFarlane, Avebury, 1982, 203 pp.
7. *Ideal Forms in the Age of Ronsard*, California University Press, 1985, i–ix, 348 pp.
8. *Moy qui me voy: the Writer and the Self from Montaigne to Leiris*, ed. with G. Craig, Oxford University Press, 1989, 229 pp.
9. *The Court Ballet of Louis XIII*, London, Victoria & Albert Museum, 1989.
10. *The Vision of Rome in the French Renaissance*, Yale University Press, 2000.
11. *Dance in the Renaissance. European Fashion: French Obsession*, Yale University Press, scheduled 2008.

B. ARTICLES

1. 'Cupid and the Bees, an Emblem in the Stirling Maxwell Collection', *Bibliotheck*, III, pp. 1–14.
2. 'The Art of withdrawal in La Fontaine's Psyché', *French Studies*, 1964, pp. 1–16.
3. 'Moral Intention in the Fables of La Fontaine', *Journal of the Warburg and Courtauld Institutes*, XXIX, 1966, pp. 164–81.
4. 'Le Papillon du Parnasse', *Australian Journal of French Studies*, IV, no. 2, pp. 204–24.
5. 'Natalie Sarraute: the Failure of an Experiment', *Studi Francesi*, XXXIII, 1967, pp. 442–8.
6. 'Prose Inspiration for Poetry: J. B. Chassignet', *The French Renaissance and its Heritage*, ed. Haggis, London, 1968, pp. 139–65.
7. 'The French Court and its Poetry', *French Literature and its Background*, ed.

J. Cruickshank, Oxford, I, 1968, pp. 63–78.

8. 'The poetry of Scève and Sponde', *French Literature and its Background'*, ed. J. Cruickshank, Oxford, I, 1968, pp. 79–97.

9. 'Ronsard', *French Literature and its Background*, ed. J. Cruickshank, Oxford, I, 1968, pp. 117–34.

10. 'La Fontaine', *French Literature and its Background*, ed. J. Cruickshank, Oxford, II, 1969, pp. 119–35.

11. 'Louis XIV and the Arts', *French Literature and its Background*, ed. J. Cruickshank, Oxford, II, 1969, pp. 82–9.

12. 'Theatres of Escape', *French Literature and its Background*, ed. J. Cruickshank, Oxford, VI, 1970, pp. 168–85.

13. 'As through a Looking-Glass: Donne's Epithalamia and their Courtly Context', *John Donne: Essays in Celebration*, ed. J. Smith, London, 1972, pp. 175–218.

14. 'Deux fêtes en Savoie en 1644 et 1645', *Baroque*, no. 5, Montauban, 1972, pp. 49–58.

15. 'The Origins of French Opera', *Oxford History of Music*, III, vol. V, 1975, pp. 169–205.

16. 'Les Jésuites à Avignon: Les fêtes au service de la propagande politique et religieuse', *Fêtes de la Renaissance*, Paris, 1975, pp. 153–71.

17. 'Racine, Menestrier and Sublime Effects', *Theatre Research*, New Series, 1976, pp. 1–11.

18. 'De Lancre's *L'Inconstance des démons*', *The Damned Art*, ed. S. Anglo, London, 1977, pp. 182–202.

19. 'Images embématiques du pouvoir royal dans la France d'Henri III', *Théorie et pratique politiques à la Renaissance*, Paris, 1977, pp. 301–21.

20. 'Gloire et recherche de soi', *Les Valeurs chez les mémorialistes français du XVIIe siècle*, ed. N. Hepp, Strasbourg, 1980, pp. 211–22.

21. 'Autour du traité du récitatif de Grimarest', *Revue du XVIIe siècle*, 1981, pp. 303–17.

22. 'Montaigne: a social role for the nobleman?', *Montaigne and his Age*, ed. K. Cameron, Exeter, 1981, pp. 86–96.

23. 'Modèles littéraires et artistiques revus par l'art et la poésie', *L'Automne de la Renaissance*, ed. A. Stegmann, Paris, 1982, pp. 309–18.

24. 'Le Ballet de cour remis au jour', *Recherche en danse*, I, 1981, pp. 33–9.

25. 'The Art of Transition in the *Essais*', *Montaigne, Essays in memory of Richard Sayce*, eds. I. D. McFarlane and I. Maclean, Oxford, 1982, pp. 35–47.

26. 'Racine's *lieu théâtral*', *Form and Meaning*, Avebury, 1982, pp. 166–87.

27. 'Literary riches from Normandy in the 17th century', *Seventeeth-century French Studies*, II, pp. 52–7.

28. 'Le rôle social de la danse au 17e siècle', *Les goûts réunis*, Paris, 1983, pp. 40–9.

29. 'Court Ballet and its Fantasies', *Seventeenth-century French Studies*, III, pp. 41–9.

30. 'The Pyrrhic; a Renaissance War Dance', *Dance Research*, 1984, pp. 29–39.

31. 'Une affaire de Famille', *Arts du Spectacle et Histoire des idées*, ed. Vaccaro,

Tours, 1984, pp. 9–20.

32. 'Le phénomène de la Galerie des Portraits des illustres', *L'Age d'or du Mécénat (1598–1661)*, Paris, 1985, pp. 411–22.

33. 'Il faut que j'aille de la plume comme des pieds', *Rhétorique de Montaigne*, Paris, 1985, pp. 165–73.

34. 'Autour d'Amphitryon', *L'Image du Souverain dans les lettres françaises*, Paris, 1985, 281–91.

35. 'La contribution du père Menestrier à la vie des fêtes en Savoie', *Culture et Pouvoir dans les Etats de Savoie*, Slatkine, 1985, pp. 129–46.

36. '*Othon* dans son contexte contemporain', *Pierre Corneille*, ed. A. Niderst, Paris, 1985, pp. 507–19.

37. Translation of Marie-Thérèse Bouquet-Boyer, "Musical Enigmas"', *Dance Research*, Spring, 1986, pp. 29–41.

38. 'An imperial flavour in some early poems of Ronsard', *Ronsard in Cambridge*, eds. P. Ford and G. Jondorf, Cambridge, 1986, pp. 26–39.

39. 'Semiotics of the dance', *Continuum*, 1986, I, pp. 243–57.

40. 'Presence of Rome in some plays of Robert Garnier', *Myth and its Making in the French Theatre*, eds. Freeman, Mason, O'Regan and Taylor, Cambridge, 1988, pp. 17–29.

41. 'Clusterings: Positive and Negative Values in *De la Vanité*', *Montaigne Studies, an Interdisciplinary Forum*, ed. P. Desan, Chicago, 1989, pp. 107–20.

42. 'Montaigne: au rebours', *Moy qui me voy*, eds. McGowan and Craig, Oxford, 1989, pp. 1–19.

43. 'La conversation de ma vie: la voix de L'Estoile dans les *Registres/Journaux*', *Travaux de Littérature*, ed. Bertaud, III, Adirel, 1990, pp. 249–60.

44. 'Le corps dansant: source d'inspiration esthétique', *Le corps à la Renaissance*, eds. Fontaine, Céard and Margolin, Paris, 1990, pp. 229–43.

45. Translation of Jérome de la Gorce, 'Guillaume-Louis Pecour', *Dance Research*, VIII, no. 2, 1990, pp. 1–26.

46. 'Contradictory Impulses in Montaigne's vision of Rome', *Renaissance Studies*, vol. 4, no. 4, 1990, pp. 392–409.

47. 'Théâtre oeuvre composite: le jeu du fantasque dans le Ballet de cour', *Création théâtrale*, ed. I. Mamczarz, Paris, 1990, pp. 53–63.

48. 'La danse: son rôle multiple', *Le Bourgeois Gentilhomme: Problèmes de la Comédie-Ballet*, ed. V. Kapp, Tübingen, 1991, pp. 163–84.

49. 'La Fonction des fêtes dans la vie de cour au XVIIe siècle', *La cour au miroir des mémorialistes, 1530–1682*, Paris, Klincksieck, Actes et colloques no. 31, 1991, pp. 27–41.

50. 'Les échanges entre le ballet et le théâtre au 17e siècle', *Les premiers opéras en Europe*, ed. I. Mamczarz, Paris, 1992, pp. 153–71.

51. 'Concordia Triumphans: l'ordre rétabli au moyen de la fête', pp. 5–25, *Chloë, Beihefte zur Daphnis*, 15, *Image et spectacles*, Actes du 37e colloque, Tours, 1988, ed. Pierre Béhar, Amsterdam, 1993.

52. 'The Arts Conjoined; a Context for the Study of Music', *Early Music History*, no. 13, ed. I. Fenlon, Cambridge University Press, 1994, pp. 171–98.

53. 'Une fête en Lorraine, 1627', *Jacques Callot, 1592–1635*, ed. D. Ternois, Paris, 1994, pp. 333–54.

54. 'Pierre de *L'Estoile*: Amateur collector of Medals and Coins', *Seventeenth-century French Studies*, vol. XV, 1993, pp. 115–27.

55. 'L'Eloge et la discrétion chez La Fontaine', *Le Fablier*, no. 5, 1993, pp. 23–30.

56. 'Impaired vision: the experience of Rome in Renaissance France', *Renaissance Studies*, vol. 8, no. 3, 1994, pp. 244–55.

57. 'L'Hyperbole dans les *Essais* de Montaigne', *Montaigne et la rhétorique*, eds. O'Brien, Quainton and Supple, Paris, 1995, pp. 99–114.

58. 'Réjouissances de Mariage; 1559, France-Savoie', pp. 177–89, *Claudin le Jeune et son temps: En France et dans les états de Savoie, 1530–1600*, ed. Marie-Thérèse Bouquet-Boyer and Pierre Bonniffet, Peter Lang, 1996.

59. 'Conjecture, reshaping and the creative process', *Michigan Romance Studies*, 1996, pp. 215–40.

60. 'Guez de Balzac: the enduring influence of Rome', *Ethics and Politics. Essays offered to Derek Watts*, eds. K. Cameron and E. Woodrough, Exeter University Press, 1996, pp. 41–64.

61. 'Ronsard's Integrated Worlds: Readings of the *Amours* (1552–3), no. xxxvii', in *The Art of Reading; Essays in memory of Dorothy Gabe Coleman*, Cambridge, 1998, pp. 35–45.

62. 'Writing down Rome at the end of the seventeenth century', *L'Invitation au voyage. Studies in honour of Peter France*, ed. John Renwick, Oxford, Voltaire Foundation, 2000, pp. 56–63.

63. 'L'art du décousu et la part du lecteur dans les *Essais*', pp. 39–50, *Lire les 'Essais' de Montaigne*, ed. J. J. Supple, Paris, Champion, 2000.

64. 'The Art of the Dance in Seventeenth-Century French Ballet de cour', *Terpsichore 1450–1900*, The Institute for Historical Dance Practice, ed. B. Ravelhofer, Ghent, 2000, conference in Ghent, 10–18 April, 2000, pp. 93–104.

65. 'The Renaissance Triumph and its Classical inheritance', pp. 26–47, *European Court Festival: Art, Politics and Performance*, ed. J. R. Mulryne, Ashgate, 2000.

66. 'Le Ballet en France et en Savoie: ses effets et son Public, 1650–1660', *Les Noces de Pélée et de Thétis*, Peter Lang, New York, 2001, pp. 1–20.

67. 'Ballets for the Bourgeois', *Dance Research*, Vol. XIX, no. 2, Winter 2001, pp. 106–26.

68. 'Montaigne and Involuntary Memory: ways of recollecting Rome', pp. 213–26, *Renaissance Reflections. Essays offered in honour of C. A. Mayer*, eds. Pauline M. Smith and Trevor Peach, Slatkine, 2002; German version 'Unwillkürliches Gedächtnis-Rom-Erfahrungen in der Spät-Renaissance', pp. 17–30, in *Ruinenbilder*, eds. Aleida Assmann, Minika Gomille, Gabriele Rippl. Hrsg. Verlag, 2002.

69. Translation of Jürgen Grimm, 'François Ogier', *Dance Research*, vol. XX, no. 2, Winter, 2002, pp. 27–37.

70. Review article of Peter N. Miller, *Peiresc's Europe, Learning & Virtue in the*

Seventeenth Century, New Haven & London, Yale University Press, 2000, in *Renaissance Studies*, vol. 16, no. 1, March 2002, pp. 100–3.

71. Review article of Benoit Bolduc, *Andromède au rocher; fortune théâtrale d'une image en France et en Italie, 1587–1712*, Florence, 2002, in *Music & Letters*, vol. 84, no. 3, August, 2003, pp. 481–3.

72. 'The Diverse Faces of Caesar: Fabrication and Manipulation in the *Essais*', *The Changing Face of Montaigne*, eds. K. Cameron and Laura Willett, Paris, Champion, 2003, pp. 121–37.

73. 'Recollections of Dancing Forms from Sixteenth-century France', *Dance Research*, vol. XXI, no. 1, Summer 2003, pp. 10–27.

74. 'Festivals and the Arts on Henri III's Journey from Cracow to Paris', in *Europa Triumphans*, eds. J. R. Mulryne and Helen Watanabe-O'Kelly, Ashgate, 2004.

75. 'Caesar's Cloak. Diversion as an art of persuasion in sixteenth-century writing', *Renaissance Studies*, Vol. 18, no. 3, September 2004, pp. 437–49.

76. 'L'Essor du ballet à la cour de Henri III', in *Henri III mécène des arts, des sciences et de l'architecture*, eds. G. Poirier, J. Maillard and I. Conihout (Paris, 2006), pp. 81–91.

77. 'The French Royal Entry in the Renaissance: the Status of the Printed Text', *French Ceremonial Entries in the Sixteenth Century*, eds. Hélène Visentin and Nicolas Russell (publication summer 2007).

78. Festivities for the mariage of Henri de Navarre & Marguerite de Valois (1572): aesthetic triumphs & political exploitation', ed. Sarah Alyn Stacey, Droz, 2007.

79. 'Dance in sixteenth and early seventeenth century France', *Dance, Spectacle, and the Body Politick, 1250–1750*, ed. Jennifer Nevile, Indiana University Press, 2008.

80. 'Fêtes: Religious and Political conflict dramatised. The role of Charles IX', *Writers in conflict in sixteenth-century France*, eds. Elizabeth Vinestock and David Foster, Durham University Press, 2007.

EU Authorised Representative:

Easy Access System Europe Mustamäe tee 50, 10621 Tallinn, Estonia

gpsr.requests@easproject.com

Printed and bound by CPI Group (UK) Ltd, Croydon, CR0 4YY

09/06/2025

01897301-0002